Simon has done Christians (and other interested people) a real service in writing this short book about the unseen spiritual world and the creatures that inhabit it. It is Biblical (for how else can we know the truth about such things), sane (which is rare for a book focussed on such matters), clear (which is wonderful for people like me), courageous (needed given the confidence with which ignorant people can speak) and applied (which is what all truth should be). Thank you, Simon.

Tim Thorburn,
Western Australia Regional Director for the Australian
Fellowship of Evangelical Students (AFES) and
Executive Officer of the Perth Gospel Partnership (PGP)

Fear Not gives wise and practical explanations of how this aspect of the Bible's teaching should—and shouldn't—affect the way we live each day as servants of the Lord Jesus. I hope that many people will read it—and I am quite sure that everybody who does will be glad they did.

Except from the Foreword by Allan Chapple,
Honorary Research Fellow and
Former Senior Lecturer (New Testament) at
Trinity Theological College, Perth, Western Australia.

Fear Not

What the Bible has to say
about angels, demons,
the occult and Satan

SIMON VAN BRUCHEM

Published by Written for our Instruction

www.writtenforourinstruction.com

Copyright © Simon van Bruchem 2020

The moral right of the author has been asserted in accordance with the Copyright Amendment (Moral Rights) Act 2000.

All rights reserved. Except as permitted under the Australian Copyright Act 1968 (for example, fair dealing for the purposes of study, research, criticism or review) no part of this publication may be reproduced, stored in a retrieval system, or transmitted in any form or by any means, electronic, mechanical, photocopying, recording or otherwise, without the written permission of the publisher.

A catalogue record for this work is available from the National Library of Australia

https://www.nla.gov.au/collections

Title: Fear Not

Subtitle: What the Bible has to say about angels, demons, the occult, and Satan

Author: van Bruchem, Simon (1978–)

ISBNs: 978-0-6489934-0-7 (paperback)
978-0-6489934-1-4 (ebook – epub)
978-0-6489934-2-1 (ebook – mobi)

Subjects: RELIGION: Biblical Reference/Handbooks; Christian Living/Spiritual Warfare; Christian Theology/Angelology & Demonology; Christian Theology/General

Cover concept by Simon van Bruchem

Cover layout by Ally Mosher at allymosher.com

Cover images under licence from Envato Elements

*Dedicated to my wife Andrea,
for whom I thank God as we
face the challenges of the visible
and invisible world together.*

Contents

Foreword .... **xi**

Introduction: The world we cannot see **1**
   The unseen world in the Bible 5
   Opening our eyes 8
   Why is it useful to understand this topic? 10
      Questions for reflection or discussion 12

Chapter 1: Angels, the Messengers of God **13**
   A brief overview of angels in the Bible 16
   A debateable angelic appearance in the Bible:
      Genesis 6 20
   Some passing references to angels we'd like
      more information about 21
   What are angels like? 29
   Are there different types of angels? 31
   What do angels do? 33
   Are there angels looking after specific areas or
      people? 36
   Do all Christians believe the same things
      about angels? 38
   A warning concerning angels 39
   Our expectation and understanding of angels ... 40
   How does it help to have a better
      understanding of angels? 41
      Questions for reflection or discussion 43

Chapter 2: Satan, the Deceiver **45**
   Different names for the devil 47

A brief overview of Satan in the Bible 49
Other passages about the devil in the Bible 55
What does the devil do? 58
Where did the devil come from? 58
What power does the devil have? 59
God can use the plans of the devil for his own
    good purposes 61
How should believers think about Satan? 62
A life trusting Jesus is a life free from the
    accusations of the devil 64
The strong man is bound: the ultimate
    encouragement 66
    Questions for reflection or discussion 69

**Chapter 3: Evil Spirits and Demon
Possession 71**
A brief overview of evil spirits in the Bible 74
Different words used of demon possession 81
Does demon possession still happen today? 82
Should Christians be afraid of evil spirits? 85
Should identification of evil spirits and
    exorcism be a part of Christian ministry
    and counselling? 87
A reminder: the evil spirits are no match for
    Jesus 89
    Questions for reflection or discussion 90

Chapter 4: Spiritual Warfare 91
The context: the flow of the book of Ephesians ... 94
Ephesians 6: the whole armour of God 97
Is there a danger in being too focused on
    spiritual warfare? 103
    Questions for reflection or discussion 106

Chapter 5: Don't Mess with the Unseen World 107
The Old Testament 110

A longer passage on this theme: Saul and the witch of En-Dor 114
The New Testament 116
Who are practitioners of the occult actually communicating with? 118
How is using prayer and the Bible different from accessing the occult? 120
Is all of this medium and fortune teller stuff a hoax? 122
Is there any harm in dabbling in tarot or visiting a medium? 123
Can we take part in festivals and cultural events involving spirits and the dead? 125
How much weight should we place on dreams? 126
How about seeking God's will by seeking out prophets, signs, or feelings of peace? 128
The need to use our wisdom and God's revelation together 129
Magic and entertainment 130
   Questions for reflection or discussion 133

Conclusion: Having Confidence in the Darkness: Jesus Is Lord 135

Acknowledgments 141

Endnotes 143

About the Author 149

Foreword

Many Christians steer well clear of the topic of this book because they find it either too weird or too threatening. But there are some who find it fascinating and give it far too much attention, and they often end up in the grip of what is little more than superstition.

What kind of guidebook would give us the help we need?

It would come to the Bible as the completely true and trustworthy word of God, and explain clearly what it teaches us about these things. But it would need to do more than discuss all of the relevant passages: it would need to show us how what they teach fits together—and also how all of this is connected to the great central truths of the gospel, concerning the glory and grace of our Lord Jesus Christ.

It would also need to give wise and practical explanations of how this aspect of the Bible's teaching should—and shouldn't—affect the way we live each day as servants of the Lord Jesus.

Finally, it would do us all a great favour if it could do all of these things in a book that wasn't too big!

That is exactly the kind of guidebook Simon has written! So I hope that many people will read it—and I am quite sure that everybody who does will be glad they did.

Allan Chapple,
Honorary Research Fellow and
Former Senior Lecturer (New Testament) at
Trinity Theological College, Perth, Western Australia.

Introduction:
The world we cannot see

There is more to this world than what we can see and touch.

Most cultures around the world have some sort of belief in an unseen world, in spirits both friendly and malevolent. In the modern Western world, the level of belief and interest in the supernatural is growing. Movies and television shows commonly feature supernatural themes involving ghosts, vampires, zombies and the underworld. For all the focus on science and rationalism in our education system, there is still longing and fascination with things that provide mystery beyond what we usually see and touch and experience. Perhaps there is an unseen world around us? Perhaps angels and demons do exist?

Angels and demons turn up in many places in modern popular culture. Bumper stickers affirm to us that angels exist. TV shows and advertising almost universally depict angels wearing white robes, having large wings, and living lives involving fluffy clouds and harps. Demons have goat legs, little horns, and pitchforks against a backdrop of flames. They feature in both comedies and in horror, used for anything from selling cream cheese to terrifying us with fears of demon possession.

The Bible says a lot about this topic, and what it says is poles apart from the popular understanding. The Bible instructs us that the world does include angels, demons, Satan, and forces beyond our control. Many modern Bible scholars dismiss this part of Bible teaching on philosophical grounds. They claim that the supernatural cannot be real, therefore the writers of the Bible must have been mistaken, and we can safely ignore the teaching on this topic.

This does not do justice to the Bible's teaching. There are a remarkable number of passages in the Bible that address the topics of angels, demons, and the underworld, sometimes directly, but more often in an indirect manner. Rather than waste time dealing with what is unknowable, the focus will be on what we can know for sure through God's word.

My interest in this topic did not start because I have had a personal experience with angels or because I have dealt with demon possession in my ministry. I believe that the Bible is the Word of God and is useful for teaching, instructing, rebuking and training in righteousness (2 Tim 3:16). There are many books and blogs out there which instruct Christians to be involved in spiritual warfare, to pray against territorial spirits, and to cast out demons. There is a lot of teaching that goes far beyond the Bible into the realm of speculation (if I am kind) or sheer fantasy (if I am not). There is a need for sanity and wisdom when it comes to this issue. The Bible has a lot to say on this topic if we would only listen; all I hope to achieve with this book is for all of us to listen well. If we do, we will grow in our knowledge of Christ and more fully appreciate his saving work on the cross.

The unseen world in the Bible

Like everyone else, I am a product of the world I have grown up in. I have grown up in the Western world, been educated as a scientist, and would like to consider myself to be a logical thinker. Because of this, when I come across mentions of angels and demons in the Bible, I cannot help but be sceptical[1]. It is beyond my personal experience. Without thinking, I have often skipped these references to focus on other parts in which I feel more comfortable.

In more recent times I have come to realize that this will not do. For example, let me point out how prominent the theme of angels and demons is in the first few chapters of the Gospel of Mark:

- Immediately after his baptism, Jesus was driven into the wilderness "being tempted by Satan. And he was with the wild animals, and the angels were ministering to him." (Mk 1:13)

- The first specific episode recorded for us in Jesus' public ministry involved Jesus casting an "unclean spirit" out of a man in the synagogue in Capernaum. (Mk 1:26)

- Jesus healed many people, "all who were sick or oppressed by demons." (Mk 1:31) There is a distinction made between the physically sick and those oppressed with demons, and it is specified that Jesus "would not permit the demons to speak, because they knew him." (Mk 1:34)

- Jesus went on to Galilee, where Mark tells us he was "preaching in their synagogues and casting out demons." (Mk 1:39)

- In the healings of chapter 3, again the "unclean spirits" are mentioned as identifying Jesus. (Mk 3:11-12)

- There is an interchange between Jesus and some scribes from Jerusalem in chapter 3 as to how Jesus can cast out demons (Mk 3:22-27). The scribes asserted it was a demonic power, while Jesus explained that he was binding the strong man (the devil) and plundering his possessions. What was not under debate was whether such demonic activity and casting out was real or not; all involved in the debate accepted that it was.

- Jesus interacts with the man who identifies himself as Legion in Mark

5:1-20. Jesus casts out the demons into nearby pigs, and the man is fully healed.

- Jesus sent out his disciples and "gave them authority over the unclean spirits" (Mk 6:12). They "cast out many demons and anointed with oil many who were sick and healed them." (Mk 6:13)

That is a great many references to spirits, angels, and demons in only six short chapters[2]. Although the main focus is clearly the identity of Jesus and his authority in many different realms, the unseen world is a common but secondary theme.

Many of the references are fleeting, tantalizing us without giving us all the answers we might like to have. For example, what might it mean for the angels to minister to Jesus after his temptation? Where do the evil spirits come from? How did people know for sure whether someone was physically sick or possessed by a demon? Or, to look more widely in the Bible, why should women wear head coverings "because of the angels" (1 Cor 11:10)? What might Jesus have meant by saying that his disciples should not despise the little ones because "in heaven, their angels always see the face of my Father who is in heaven"? (Matt. 18:10)

I wish I could claim that this book will definitively answer all of these questions, but it cannot.

Angels and demons are not the focus of the Bible's teaching most of the time but appear at the fringes of the story. Peter Bolt describes the spiritual world as being similar to a criminal network such as the Mafia: we know that they are there, operating in our cities, yet most of us do not come into contact with them or know much about them[3]. We cannot know all that we would like to know during our time on earth, and that is fine. In fact, I would argue that this is good for us. We would like to satisfy our curiosity about all kinds of issues, but God has told us all that we need to know for life and godliness in the Bible (2 Peter 1:3). We are to listen well to what we are told, but we are not told everything.

Opening our eyes

The unseen world of angels and demons does exist. Most of the time humans are unaware of anything beyond what we can experience with our senses, but there are certain times when the unseen world is revealed to people.

In 2 Kings 6, the prophet Elisha was frustrating the plans of the king of Syria in his attempts to defeat the army of Israel. In response, the Syrian army surrounded the city of Dothan where Elisha and his servant were staying. Elisha's servant woke the next day to see the city surrounded and he was afraid. His master Elisha responded by encouraging him that "those who are with us are more than those who are with them." Elisha prayed for God to open the eyes of his servant so he could see what usually cannot be seen. And God did:

> *"So the LORD opened the eyes of the young man, and he saw, and behold, the mountain was full of horses and chariots of fire all around Elisha."*
>
> (2 Kings. 6:17)[4]

Although angels are not mentioned by name here, the usual interpretation is that they are seeing the heavenly army of the Lord. They were always present, and Elisha the prophet was aware of them, but his servant needed to have his eyes opened by God to see them.

There are many occasions in the Bible when people come into contact with angels or the spiritual world. Sometimes it is immediately obvious that something supernatural is going on like when the shepherds were confronted with the heavenly host in Luke 2, or the locals are confronted with demonic power in the person of Legion in Mark 5. But in many of the accounts, those who saw angels or who were opposed by the devil were unaware at the time. Balaam did not see the angel standing in the road in front of him until the LORD opened his eyes (Numbers 22:31). Gideon had a long conversation with a man not realizing that he was an angel until the angel consumed the food placed before him with fire (Judges 6:22). Indeed, the writer to the Hebrews encourages hospitality to strangers, noting that some have entertained angels without knowing it (Hebrews 13:2).

We should be aware that the physical world is not all there is. All of us have a tendency to think of ourselves more highly than we ought to. We focus on ourselves, or our family, or our tribe. If considering this topic does nothing else, it should open our eyes to the fact that the universe God made is much bigger than this. With eyes of faith, we can see a bigger picture.

Why is it useful to understand this topic?

There are right and wrong motivations to want to know more about angels and demons. Some want to understand the unseen world because they are terrified of things that go bump in the night and are afraid of what might be out there. Others are fascinated with the topic and end up obsessed with it, a danger that dates back to Biblical times. Still others wish to explore the possibility of contacting loved ones who have died or of foretelling the future.

Christians should understand at least a little about the unseen world because God has revealed it to us in the Bible; there is a great deal we can know because we have been told. As we look into what is revealed to us more deeply, the result should be that Christians are even more assured of the power of Jesus and the secure position we have in Christ. There are many understandings of the unseen world in the wider culture, and we need to know the reality so as not to be distracted by the false fantasies peddled by many.

It will help you to read this book with a Bible by your side. As we read and draw conclusions, we will see how knowing these things helps build our faith and keeps us focused on the One with real power in the seen and unseen universe: Jesus.

Questions for reflection or discussion

- Have you often considered the fact that angels, demons, and Satan are real? Why/why not?

- Why do you think that supernatural themes feature so heavily in modern culture that is generally secular and non-religious?

- What would you like to know about the unseen world? Make a list before reading the rest of this book. How do you think it would benefit you to know these things?

Chapter 1:
Angels, the Messengers of God

Angels turn up in popular culture in all kinds of odd places. They are often minor characters in movies and TV shows and have even been used to sell ice cream and cream cheese. Angels also feature heavily in Christmas decorations. If asked to describe what an angel looks like, many people would draw a woman in a long white robe with wings and a halo. The wings are what would make most of us think 'angel' rather than 'woman in a white dress'.

According to the Bible, almost all of our usual expectations of angels are incorrect. Wings are rarely mentioned, haloes never are, and their gender is never defined. The angels of the Bible are not docile and domesticated but are beings of great power. It is clear that we need the Bible to provide us with a more accurate understanding of what angels are really like.

The word translated *angel* in both Hebrew and Greek simply means *messenger*. It is not a word that is only used to describe heavenly beings, though most of the uses that we find in the Bible do refer to God's messengers. Angels do the work of God, generally delivering messages to specific people for specific purposes, but sometimes being active in judgment, rescue or guidance.

Although angelic appearances catch our attention, they are quite rare in the Biblical account. Long periods pass with no recorded angelic appearance, while at certain times the appearances are more frequent. The Bible covers an extensive time period, and although there are many angelic appearances recorded, they are unusual. God intervenes directly through angels at specific times in specific ways in the world and not as the usual method of control.

How are we going to build a more accurate understanding of angels? Firstly, we will take a stroll through the Bible and see how the teaching about angels unfolds through the Biblical storyline. Secondly, we will look at some of those strange passing references to angels in the Bible that give us glimpses of the unseen angelic realm. Finally, we will answer some key questions about angels using what we have gleaned from our investigation of the Bible's teaching.

A brief overview of angels in the Bible

Angels are described as bringing messages from God to specific people in the book of Genesis. The angel of the LORD appeared to Hagar when she fled from Sarai in Genesis 16:7, and again when she was sent away in Genesis 21:17. Abraham received three strange visitors in Genesis 18, two of whom are described as angels later on in 19:1. The angel of the LORD called to Abraham to stop the sacrifice of Isaac in Genesis 22:11. Jacob had a famous dream of angels ascending and descending on a ladder while stopping at Bethel (Genesis 28:12), and an angel spoke to Jacob later on outlining how he could leave Laban with a large flock (Genesis 31:11). Jacob wrestled with God in Genesis 32; an event later described as wrestling with an angel (Hosea 12:4).

In Exodus, angelic involvement is more varied. God spoke to Moses via an angel who appeared as a burning bush (Exodus 3:2). The pillar of fire which led the people through the wilderness in the night is described as an angel in Exodus 14:29, and other references to God leading his people also use the word 'angel' (such as Exodus 20:20 and 32:34). In the New Testament, the law is described as being delivered by angels (Acts 7:38, Galatians 3:19).

Perhaps the most amusing angelic appearance recorded in the Bible concerns the diviner Balaam in Numbers 22. The king of Moab called on Balaam to curse the Israelites who were a threat to him, and as Balaam travelled there to do this on his donkey, the donkey kept turning off the path. The LORD first opened the mouth of the donkey to speak to his owner before opening Balaam's eyes to see the angel of the LORD "standing in the way, with his drawn sword in his hand." (Numbers 22:31) The angel opposed Balaam's mission and redirected him to bless the Israelites, which is what Balaam ended up doing.

Angels are described as commissioning several of the judges, including Gideon (Judges 6) and Samson (Judges 13).

In many of these passages, the message delivered by the angel is described as being the LORD himself speaking. For example, in the account of the commissioning of Gideon, although we are told that he is speaking to an angel, it is also described at times as him speaking with the LORD (Judges 6:16). The angels simply deliver the message from God, as if God himself were speaking it.

Angels are also described as delivering God's judgment. A message of judgement was delivered to the people in the times of the judges via an angel (Judges 2:1-4), and God's judgement on Israel because of David's census was delivered by an angel (2 Samuel 24). In the biggest and most famous case, the angel of the LORD struck down 185 000 Assyrians who were besieging Jerusalem in 2 Kings 19:35[5].

It's not all judgment and messages though; angels also act at specific times to save God's people. Both the extra man in the fiery furnace and the rescue from the lion's den are ascribed to the work of angels (Daniel 3:28, 6:22).

The angels of God were thought to have been incredibly pure and wise, as seen in the common language of the people by the time of Samuel.

Achish of the Philistines described David as being "as blameless in [his] sight as an angel of God" (1 Samuel 29:9), and the woman of Tekoa described David as being as wise as an angel of God (2 Samuel 14:20).

In apocalyptic books like the latter parts of Daniel and the book of Revelation, angels are described as the guides through the revealed world. They are the ones who explain what is happening and why. Angels also feature heavily in Daniel and Revelation as those who carry out the will of God, often in judgment or in worship.

We see the most angelic appearances in quick succession in the accounts of Jesus' birth in Matthew and Luke. Angels appear in dreams to Joseph (Matthew 1:20,24, 2:13,19) and in person to Zechariah and Mary (Luke 1:11, 26). Angels famously appear in a heavenly host to the shepherds outside Bethlehem (Luke 2:9-15). Angels also appear at the resurrection (Matthew 28) and the ascension of Jesus (Acts 1:10).

Jesus' teaching adds to our understanding of angels. They will be involved in the final judgment (Matthew 13:39), returning with Jesus at his second coming (Matthew 16:27). There are massive numbers of angels who God could call at any time (Matthew 26:53). Angels are present with God, celebrating when people enter the kingdom (Luke 15:10).

Angels directed the gospel expansion to the Ethiopian (Acts 8:26) and to the Gentiles through Cornelius (Acts 10). An angel released Peter from prison (Acts 12:7) and struck down Herod with worms (Acts 12:23). During a storm at sea, Paul saw an angel who assured him of his safety (Acts 27:23).

However powerful angels might be, the consistent encouragement is that angels, like the rest of the created order, are under God's control (1 Peter 3:22). Several passages include warnings not to worship angels (Colossians 2:18, Hebrews 1, Revelation 19:10). There are a number of passing references to angels in other New Testament letters, though they tend to be on the fringes of the apostles' teaching rather than the main point.

A debateable angelic appearance in the Bible: Genesis 6

In Genesis 6 we are told that "the sons of God" saw the "daughters of man" as attractive and had children by them. In the immediate context, these unions are an illustration of the growing wickedness on the earth which God then punished with the flood. A common ancient interpretation of these verses was that the "sons of God" here is speaking of angels, and the mating of angels with people was abhorrent to God[6]. Those who hold to this way of reading

Genesis 6 believe that the apostle Peter is speaking of this episode in 2 Peter 2:4 and Jude is referring to it in Jude 1:6.

I feel that this interpretation is not the best way to read Genesis 6. The phrase "sons of God" is used of angels in other places, but is not commonly applied to them. It seems that in the immediate context, following the covenant line genealogy in Genesis 5, the "sons of God" most naturally refers to the people in the covenant line of promise. If this is right, then the intermarriage of the covenant people with others is a sign of the growing wickedness in the world, which would be consistent with later prohibitions in the law.

As for the references in 2 Peter and Jude, there is nothing in them that definitively links them to Genesis 6. They could refer to the fall of Satan and his angels instead of Genesis 6, something we will explore later in this book.

Another factor against the presence of angels in Genesis 6 is that Jesus himself says that angels do not marry and are not sexual beings (Matthew 23:30).

Some passing references to angels we'd like more information about

Many of the references to angels in the Bible are tantalizing and brief, side comments by the Biblical writers that are not explained as deeply as we would like. There are some conclusions we can draw from these passages, though we need to be careful not to veer into speculation or read our own understanding into the text.

Judging angels

When encouraging the Corinthian Christians not to bring lawsuits against other believers, Paul makes an interesting comment when he notes that "we are to judge angels" (1 Corinthians 6:3). This is meant as an encouragement that normal matters are well within the capability of believers to sort out. Paul never goes on to expand on his statement; in the context, we can know that this judging of angels will be part of believers judging the world at the end of time. As with some other New Testament references to angels, this shows us that people are special in God's sight, redeemed by Jesus in a way that angels are not. Indeed, Peter later tells us that the gospel of Jesus revealed to believers is something into which angels long to look (1 Peter 1:12).

Peter's angel

Acts 12 includes the account of Peter being released from prison by an angel. When the now-free Peter knocked unexpectedly on the door of the house where many believers were staying, a servant girl named Rhoda came to answer. She was so happy to see Peter that she ran to tell the others that Peter was outside, leaving poor Peter out in the cold! The response of those in the house was interesting; they kept saying, "it is his angel." (Acts 12:15). Why would they think this? There are two related ideas raised here: the idea of guardian angels and an understanding of what happens immediately after death.

This way of thinking is reflected in the ancient Christian book the Shepherd of Hermas, which teaches that each person has a guardian angel. A common understanding was that immediately after death, the angel of a person could appear for a time[7]. If this is what those in the house that night believed, it would mean that they thought Peter had been executed in prison, a far more likely event than being released by an angel. A similar thing seems to be going on in Luke 24:27 when the disciples had the risen Jesus appear suddenly among them; they thought they saw a "spirit." This idea is nowhere explained in the Bible but seemed to be a common view in the first century. The two passages referred to here are descriptive and do not mean that personal angels actually appear after someone's death. It simply means that this is what the people at that time commonly understood to be true.

Head coverings because of the angels

In the middle of Paul's discussion about head coverings in the church, we come across a curious verse:

> *"That is why a wife ought to have a symbol of authority on her head, because of the angels."*

(1 Corinthians 11:10)

Just as with the previous reference to people judging angels, Paul never expands on this idea. It is not the only reason he gives in support of head coverings for women during prayer, but it is a fascinating reference. The respected commentator Anthony Thiselton notes that this cannot be linked to the sons of God passage in Genesis 6, but other than that there is nothing we can be certain of. One possibility which makes sense is that the angels are 'watchers of created order' and are concerned with things being done rightly and in order in God's world. Another possibility would be that because believing women will one day be among those who judge angels, they should now have the wisdom to exercise freedom correctly to maintain order in public worship[8]. We do not have enough information to be certain; it is one of those passages which will remain somewhat unclear this side of heaven.

The angels of the little ones in Matthew 18

In Matthew 18, Jesus uses a small child to illustrate how important the "little ones" are to God. He warns the disciples that causing any "little one" who believes in him to sin would lead to a terrible consequence. Then after a warning not to despise the "little ones," Jesus says:

> *"For I tell you that in heaven their angels always see the face of my Father who is in heaven"*

(Matthew 18:10b)

This verse that has led to much speculation for it raises some interesting questions. It does seem that the word 'angels' here is speaking of supernatural beings and not messengers of another type. But what can it mean when Jesus mentions "their angels"? Does every believer have their own angel? This is where the idea of a guardian angel comes from as there are no other verses in the Bible that speak of this concept in any clear way. John Calvin, who was always incredibly careful not to speculate on what the Bible does not expand upon, cautiously said that this verse does appear to speak about guardian angels[9]. However, without any further information, we don't know any details about this as God has chosen not to inform us. It fits with the wider Biblical teaching that God cares for and looks after every one of his children (Matthew 6:26).

Another interesting possibility is that Jesus might be saying that the angels of the 'little ones' are actually in a superior position to the angels of others because they always see the face of God directly. Again, there is no explicit contrast here with the angels of others, and we would be speculating beyond the text to affirm this with any confidence. It is enough to say that Jesus is encouraging his disciples (and us) that even the believer who seems least important is of incredible value to God.

The law delivered by angels

By New Testament times it was common to describe the Old Testament law as being given to Moses by angels. This was not explicitly stated in the Old Testament, but it was a reasonable inference based on their theology at the time. God was so holy and pure and transcendent that he needed a mediator; no-one could see him face to face (John 1:14). God must, therefore, have delivered the message the way he delivered other important messages, using angels. Saying that the law was delivered by angels is a way of not only speaking of the need for mediation with a holy God but also a way of showing the importance of the law. Stephen speaks of the role of angels in delivering the law (Acts 7:38, 53), as does Paul (Galatians 3:19) and the writer to the Hebrews (Hebrews 2:2).

Tongues of men or of angels

In 1 Corinthians 13, Paul mentions the "tongues of men or of angels" in v1. Although this is a passing reference, it has been used to justify many different types of tongue speaking in church. The main point of Paul's message here is that speaking in tongues was the use of real languages that the speaker had not learned, which needed to be interpreted to be useful to the wider congregation. Some Christian churches continue to use ecstatic utterances in corporate worship which are not understandable to those listening, justifying this activity as being the "tongues of angels" using 1 Corinthians 13:1. Ironically, this contradicts the overall teaching of 1 Corinthians 12-14. Paul is promoting understandable utterances and suppressing anything that is not understandable or interpreted; this passage cannot be used to support ecstatic utterances.

In fact, it is not at all clear that Paul is telling us that angels have a specific language or languages which are different from human languages. His purpose is not to give us information on angel linguistics! It is most likely simply an exaggeration like we might say we were "hungry enough to eat a horse." The aim of v1 is to state that however impressive the language that is used, love is the key element that needs to be present.

We see something similar in Galatians when Paul strongly defends the gospel he has preached, saying that even if an angel in heaven were to preach something different they would be accursed (Galatians 1:8). The point is not that angels might have a habit of preaching false gospels, but rather that however impressive the speaker, if the message is not that we are saved by grace through faith in Jesus alone, their message is evil and wrong

Angels ministering to Jesus

The gospels record two instances where Jesus is ministered to by angels. The first is after his confrontation with Satan in the temptation account (Mark 1:13) and the second is when an angel strengthened him in the garden of Gethsemane (Luke 22:43). At times when Jesus was especially drained he was given extra assistance in angelic form. We do not know how the angels ministered to and strengthened him, but we can know that the Father was providing for Jesus in his time of need.

It is worth noting here that Jesus chose not to call down angels to help him while being tempted (Luke 4:10). He also restrained his disciples from fighting those who arrested him by claiming that he could call on twelve legions of angels if he asked for them (Matthew 26:53). The angels at times encourage Jesus, but the mission he was on was something he needed to complete alone. He refused to call for some more convenient but incomplete victory, for only his death could save people lost in sin.

Angels can be charged with error

The reality of the devil and fallen angels is clearly taught in the Bible, a topic we will visit in detail in later chapters. Job mentions that angels can be charged with error (Job 4:18), while Peter notes that angels had sinned and were punished (2 Peter 2:4) as does Jude (Jude 1:6). The Bible doesn't provide the details of the events that led to angels falling into sin and only gives glimpses into this reality. This didn't stop writers of fiction like John Milton and Dante Alighieri filling in the gaps in vivid colour!

It is enough for us to know that angels have sinned and been punished for their sin in the past. The redemption that was won in Jesus is something that angels do not understand and is not for them (1 Peter 1:12). The victory Jesus won redeems the children of Adam and not supernatural beings.

What are angels like?

If you asked most people who came face-to-face with an angel in the Bible what they were like, the answer would be "terrifying." A common response to being confronted with an angel was to cower in fear (Luke 1:12, 26).

Wayne Grudem defines angels as "created, spiritual beings with moral judgment and high intelligence, but without physical bodies."[10] Most of the time angels are invisible to people, but God might choose to reveal them to people at specific times. Not having physical bodies as we do, they are not as limited as we are. For example, angels can appear and disappear (Judges 6), they can appear in a terrifying form (Numbers 22) or look like normal men (Genesis 18). Although the common depiction of angels in Christian artwork involves white robes and wings, wings are rarely mentioned in Biblical angelic appearances.

Angels do not have gender in the way that people do, and they are not married or given in marriage (Matthew 23:30). Our common understanding of angels being female, therefore, cannot be justified from the Bible.

They are immortal in nature rather than mortal, as we see with the angels Gabriel (Daniel 8:16, Luke 1:26) and Michael (Daniel 10:13, Jude 1:9) mentioned as being active in episodes many centuries apart.

It is important to remember that for all of their power and at times terrifying appearances, angels are creatures and not divine. They are limited in what they know (1 Peter 1:12). Despite being 'glorious ones', they do not pronounce judgment with their own authority (Jude 1:9); they are creatures of a much higher authority than themselves. There have been times where people have been tempted to worship angels, but this is universally condemned in the Bible. Paul speaks of the worship of angels as something that distracts from a focus on Christ and proper Christian growth (Colossians 2:16-19) while the writer to the Hebrews emphasizes the supremacy of Christ over angels in some detail (Hebrews 1). When the apostle John fell down to worship the angel who was guiding him in his vision, the angel rebuked him and directed him to worship God (Revelation 19:10). However impressive angels might be, they are not to be worshipped; only God is worthy of our praise.

Are there different types of angels?

There are different ranks of angels though we are not told enough in the Bible to be certain as to how this hierarchy works. In Luke 1:19, Gabriel describes himself to Zechariah as one "who stands in the presence of God," which could imply that he is of higher rank than other angels. The term 'archangel' occurs in 1 Thessalonians 4:16 and Jude 1:9 (speaking of Michael), again suggesting some ranking of the angelic host. And in John's descriptions in Revelation, he mentions "mighty angels" several times as opposed to the more usual "angels" (Revelation 5:2, 10:1, 18:21).

In addition to this, we can also read references to cherubim and seraphim, two different categories of angels.

Cherubim were placed by God to guard the garden of Eden with a flaming sword once Adam and Eve were expelled from it (Genesis 3:24). When God commanded the ark of the covenant to be built, he directed that two cherubim be placed on the cover of the ark with the wings facing one another (Exodus 25:18). God was said to be enthroned on the cherubim of the ark (1 Samuel 4:4), speaking from between them to Moses (Numbers 7:18). Later, King Solomon built two massive cherubim covered in gold in the temple and also depicted them on the doors and walls (1 Kings 6).

Despite the familiar patterns all Israelites would have seen at the temple, the prophet Ezekiel saw the cherubim for himself. The living creatures among the wheels of the mobile throne room of God in Ezekiel's vision are identified as cherubim (Ezekiel 10:2). These creatures appeared to have human form but powerful extra features. In his attempt to describe them, Ezekiel says that their likeness was "like burning coals of fire" (Ezekiel 1:13). Their role as supporting the throne of the Lord has led to much speculation about their rank and power. It is reasonable to say that Ezekiel's vision of the cherubim is the background behind the living creatures of John's vision in Revelation 4.

The seraphim, literally the "fiery ones," are only mentioned specifically in Isaiah's vision of the Lord in Isaiah 6[11]. The description we have of them is vivid: "Each had six wings: with two he covered his face, and with two he covered his feet, and with two he flew" (Isa. 6:2). They are described as standing above the Lord on his throne. Despite their exalted position and obvious power, they are creatures who serve and worship the true God constantly.

The earliest known detailed ranking of angels can be found in a book called the 'Celestial Hierarchy' written around 500AD by a man known as Pseudo-Dionysius. He proposed a series of nine angelic ranks between people and God, and this proposal was generally accepted until the middle ages where it was expanded into the full angelology of Thomas Aquinas in his Summa Theologica[12]. There is scant Biblical basis to rank angels so precisely. As we have seen, there are hints that there are angels of special position or power, but God in his wisdom has not detailed how such a ranking might operate[13].

What do angels do?

When we survey the many Bible passages that feature angels, we can categorise their actions in three key areas: worship, delivering messages, and acting as God's agents in the world.

(a) Angels constantly worship God

It is important that we get this point clear in our minds first. It is easy to become fascinated with angels because they are beyond our experience. They are mighty; they appear and disappear; it is clear that they are powerful creatures. We must not overemphasize their authority despite their great power. All angels, however great their power and position, are servants of God and worship Him.

We see this, for example, in passages like Revelation 7:11, where angels are listed as worshipping God constantly along with the multitude of the saved and the elders. The seraphim of Isaiah 6 were also described as being involved in worship constantly.

Angels might be fascinating, but the focus of our praise and attention needs to be Jesus, who is their ruler and ours.

(b) Angels can act as messengers, delivering God's word to a specific person at a specific time

Angels most commonly appear in the Bible delivering messages from God to people. After all, as we have seen, the word 'angel' means 'messenger'. As messengers, they are not inventing the message, only delivering a message from God. They are acting on behalf of God and therefore the promises they made to people always came about.

There is something important to notice here. God did deliver messages using angels, but this was an unusual way to do it. Most of the time, God spoke to his people through prophets in the Old Testament and the apostles in the New Testament. It is possible to think that because we have many accounts of angelic appearances in the Bible, therefore God often used angels to deliver messages. The reality is that over the very long time period of Biblical history, angels delivering messages were very rare. This is not God's usual method of communication with people.

Angels are usually depicted in classical Christian art as terrifying glowing figures before whom people bow down to the ground. Although this is true at times in the Biblical record, it can give the wrong impression of the relative roles of angels and people. Angels minister to people; they serve them, not rule them. Paul McPartlan points out that Leonardo da Vinci's painting of the angel appearing to Mary has Gabriel kneeling before Mary[14]. This captures the relationship in a more accurate manner and makes sense of other passages where believers are told that they will judge angels.

(c) Angels can act as God's agents in the world, bringing comfort, protection, or judgement

An agent is someone who acts on behalf of someone greater than themselves. Angels do not only deliver messages from God in the Bible; they can act in all kinds of different ways. They ministered to Jesus in the wilderness, bringing him comfort. They strengthened Jesus in the Garden of Gethsemane (Luke 22:43). They directed gospel conversations for Philip and Peter and Paul. They also protect people in some way, as pointed to by Matt 18:10.

Not all of the angelic work in the world is of a positive or comforting nature. Angels are described as acting in judgement, as in the account of Sodom and Gomorrah and the census in the time of David. They acted to bring an unexpected defeat to the Assyrian army in 2 Kings. This acting in judgement is also something they will do in the future, being involved in the work of God on judgment day[15].

The writer to the Hebrews describes angels as being "ministering spirits sent out to serve for the sake of those who are to inherit salvation" (Heb 1:14). As God works all things for the good of those who love him (Rom 8:28), he can use angels to carry out his purposes.

Are there angels looking after specific areas or people?

As discussed previously, the idea of personal guardian angels can find some support in Matthew 18, but it is not expanded on or mentioned in other places in the Bible. Paul and the other apostles never appeal to angelic guardians to work among believers or encourage believers to pray for angelic protection. If angels are protecting God's people all the time, it seems that this is something believers do not need to be overly concerned with.

In Daniel 10, God reveals that angels (named "princes" in v13, 20-21) can oversee or fight for specific areas or countries. Daniel is told about a celestial battle that he was previously unaware of. Interestingly, Daniel is not instructed to pray for a specific prince to win or to act in any way towards this celestial battle. He is not told to work out which angel might be responsible for which area or to seek out the names or functions of the angels[16]. The battle between the princes is revealed to him as an encouragement that God is working in ways he does not know and does not fully understand.

This concept of territorial angels has been expanded in the modern theology of some to include territorial evil spirits as well. In fact, some speak of a deliverance ministry where angels must be named, and the hierarchy of spiritual beings in a particular region must be discovered[17]. This kind of ministry is never encouraged in the Bible and is a distraction from what believers should be concerned with. It is right to believe in a spiritual world that we cannot see; it is something else entirely to think that we should work to influence or control this world. It is enough for us to trust that God is sovereign and is working in ways we cannot always explain.

Do all Christians believe the same things about angels?

God's people have always had a range of views about angels. Luke tells us in Acts 23:8 that the Sadducees denied the concepts of resurrection, angels, and spirits, but the Pharisees acknowledged them all. Likewise, in the modern Christian church, there are a number of views ranging from complete rejection to a strong overemphasis on the angelic host.

Today, some churches reject the supernatural on principle and therefore have no time for discussions of angels and demons, seeing them as a hangover from the past that we have moved on from in our scientific world. I believe that the Bible is the word of God and we should take what it says seriously and carefully. If you also hold to that conviction, you must believe that angels exist; they are assumed throughout the Bible.

There are some, however, especially in the Pentecostal churches, that overemphasize the angelic host. As discussed before, there are also deliverance ministries which focus on naming angels and demons. While angels are mentioned many times in the Bible, we are not encouraged to seek them out or to interact with them. God sends angels to people at specific times in the

Bible; people do not seek them out. The angelic world is revealed to certain people for specific reasons, but it is not something that all believers are told that we will experience. Such an experience is not necessary for salvation or growth in the Christian life.

A warning concerning angels

Angels are fascinating. It is encouraging to know that God has supernatural servants that do his will and protect his people.

A healthy interest must not, however, lead to an obsession. It would seem that some groups in New Testament times had focussed too heavily on angels. Some in Colossae had started to worship angels (Colossians 2:18), something that Paul describes as a distraction from Jesus. John was tempted to fall down and worship an angel in his vision in Revelation, only to be rebuked and told not to (Revelation 19:10). Angels are incredible, powerful spiritual beings; but they are creatures, like us. Worship of angels is idolatry just like the worship of any other creature (Romans 1:25).

Angels are servants of God, and God's great mission in the world is to bring all things under the headship of Jesus (Colossians 1:15-20). Jesus is superior in every way to angels (Hebrews 1) and is the only mediator between God and man (1 Timothy 2:5). Jesus is the only way to the

Father[18]; angels cannot save anyone. We should be focussed on what God has done for us and how we should respond, not distracted by a focus on angels.

Our expectation and understanding of angels

This chapter might have given the impression that angels are an everyday kind of occurrence for believers because there are so many references to them in the Bible. This is not the case. Remember that the Bible covers a time period of thousands of years! On that scale, angelic appearances are rare. Many generations passed with no angelic appearance. In fact, the appearances that we have recorded for us are written down *because* they are unusual.

Importantly, Jesus and the apostles do not encourage believers to seek out angels. As much as we might want God to speak to us personally with a special message or a mission for our lives, this is not something God promises to us. What God has revealed to us through his word is enough.

As Moses says in Deuteronomy 29:29, "the secret things belong to the LORD our God, but the things that are revealed belong to us and to our children forever, that we may do the words of this law." Instead of striving uselessly to find out details that we cannot know, we have God's written word to instruct us, to read, know and follow.

How does it help to have a better understanding of angels?

After all of our investigation into the Biblical view of angels, the conclusion that we are not to seek out angels or expect them to reveal themselves to us might be a bit of a disappointment. Is there any real value in knowing that angels exist and what they are like if we, most likely, will not encounter them in this life?

Yes, there is. Think of it like this: when you were a small child, your understanding of the world was small as well. When you were a baby, you initially started to understand what your own body was, who your family were, what your room looked like, and what your house was like. Over time, your understanding of the world grew. You learnt about your neighbourhood, your wider relatives and your school. You saw the sun during the day and the stars at night. At some point, it was explained to you that the sun is much bigger than you expected and much further away, and that amazed and fascinated you. Then you learnt about the solar system and how the earth is the perfect location for life, designed just as it needed to be. And then you saw pictures from the Hubble telescope of other planets ridiculously long distances away. Even then, of course, there was more to know. You learnt that the solar system we live in is small compared to the universe, which is so large it defies description. As your understanding of the universe grew, you should also grow in wonder at the One who made all of it. The whole universe was always there, but you discovered more about it as you grew up. The statement "God created the heavens and the earth" starts to have greater meaning as you understand just how extensive the heavens are.

It is similar as we start to understand the reality of angels and other beings in the unseen world. They were always there, a whole spiritual realm that we rarely see and often do not understand. As we grow in our understanding of this unseen world and understand with new eyes that this world is far more than what we usually experience, we should be more appreciative of how powerful our God really is. God made all of this. He controls all of this. And Jesus is Lord of all of this.

The reality of angels reminds us that God is far more powerful and so much greater than we usually imagine. He has sent angels to specific people to progress his perfect plan for the world at specific times. That should be a marvellous encouragement.

Questions for reflection or discussion

- How does the Biblical view of angels differ from the angels that are depicted in modern advertising and television?

- Do you find knowing the power and influence of angels in the world comforting?

- How might believing in the ministry of angels give us a better understanding of God's power?

- Angels delivered messages or judgment from God to his people at certain times and places in history. Should we expect God to speak to us this way? Why/why not?

Chapter 2:
Satan, the Deceiver

"The greatest trick the devil ever pulled was convincing the world he didn't exist."

Kaiser Sose, The Usual Suspects[19]

Satan, also referred to as the devil, is for many people the equivalent of the bogeyman or the monster under the bed. He is the trump card that parents conjure up to scare their children into obedience. The threat of some supernatural being with incredible power to inflict punishment and cause evil may have kept people from immoral behaviour in the past, but surely we have moved on from this in the modern world?

The Bible disagrees. Satan is real. The devil has the power to cause misery and pain and is not a being to be mocked or ignored. Admittedly, as we saw with angels in the previous chapter, references to Satan are not that common and not always as clear as we would like. However, the overall picture the Bible paints for us of the devil is sobering, and all Christians should have at least a basic understanding of who the devil is and why this matters.

Different names for the devil

The word *Satan* is not actually a name but a title. *Satan* can be literally translated as something like adversary, opponent, or enemy[20]. He opposes the rule of God in the world.

This being goes by a range of names in the Bible, each of them conveying an aspect of his character:

- The word *devil* means slanderer or accuser[21]. This is the most common title used in the New Testament.

- The name *Lucifer* originates from the Latin translation of the Bible, the Vulgate, from Isaiah 14:12-14. Most modern translations translate the word *Lucifer* as "morning star" (as in the ESV) but the title *Lucifer* remained in the King James Version. This passage speaks of the fall of the devil from his previous exalted position. He could once have been referred to as the morning star, a being with great power and beauty, but this title no longer applies to him. This makes Lucifer somewhat of an ironic title, as it refers to a being of great evil in terms of beauty and wonder.

- *Beelzebul* is a term used of the devil in the gospel accounts of Jesus binding the strong man, where Jesus was accused of casting out demons by the prince of demons (Luke 11:15, Matt 10:25). Scholars are divided as to the origin of this name. It could translate as "Lord of Dung" from the Aramaic word for adversary, or it could mean "Lord of the dwelling" which would make sense as Jesus speaks of the house of Beelzebul[22].

Whatever name is ascribed to this being, it is clear that there is a hierarchy of demons and evil spirits that answer to a ruler. This ruler is named the "prince of demons" (Luke 11:15) or the "prince of the power of the air" (Ephesians 2:2). Satan is the ruler of the demonic world.

A brief overview of Satan in the Bible

Job

The Old Testament only contains a few direct references to the devil, of which the most prominent may be found in the first two chapters of Job. These chapters speak of the time when God allows Satan to bring suffering into the life of Job with the intention of testing him to see if Job would curse God (Job 1:11). A series of terrible tragedies then happened to Job's family and possessions, but Job did not sin or charge God with wrong (Job 1:22), Satan presented himself to God once more (Job 2:1), and this time God allowed Satan to attack Job physically as long as his life was spared (Job 2:6). Job did not sin in all of this, despite being covered with loathsome sores (Job 2:7-10), and at this point Satan leaves the account of Job, never to return. The interaction between God and Satan gives us insight into Job's suffering, something that was never revealed to Job himself. In God's awesome answer to Job in chapters 38-41, he never mentions Satan's role in Job's suffering but places emphasis on God's power and sovereignty as something that Job can never see or fully understand.

The account of Satan in Job 1-2 reveals some interesting facts about the devil. Satan is unable to bring suffering on Job without the permission of God. It is clear that the world is not dualistic, like in Taoist philosophy, with good and evil in equal proportions and with equal power. No, God is completely in control of what happens to Job and nothing happens without his permission. God does use different means to carry out his purposes in the world, including, it would seem, even allowing the malicious work of the devil[23]. The devil only has evil intent for Job and for his relationship with God, but God uses even this evil intent to bring about his own glory and a deeper understanding for Job.

There are many things we would like to know more about from the account of Job 1-2. Does Satan regularly present himself before God? Why is Satan in the heavenly council at all? Why does God allow Satan to do what he does? With this final issue, we can conclude that God is more interested in his glory than our comfort; suffering can produce good fruit and ultimately be beneficial for us (as in 1 Peter 1:6-7).

The rest of the Old Testament

David's tragic census in 2 Samuel 24 led to a terrible judgment that killed thousands of God's people. In this account, the census was provoked by God's anger inciting David to act in this way. In the parallel account in 1 Chronicles 1, we read that Satan incited David to take the census. However, in both cases, David himself is revealed as guilty of great sin that requires atonement. How might these seemingly contradictory accounts be resolved? Considering what we have already seen in Job will help us here. God remains in control of all that happens, both good and evil, so it would be correct to see God's hand in this action as the writer of 2 Samuel does. However, God does allow Satan certain power in the world, so 1 Chronicles is also a correct description of what happened. Whether we attribute the inciting to God or Satan here, David maintains responsibility for his actions. He is in no position to say "the devil made me do it" or "the Spirit provoked me;" he is guilty of sin. Satan is depicted here as one who tempts people to do evil, a common theme in the other Bible passages we will look at.

The only other direct mention of Satan in the Old Testament is in the vision of the prophet Zechariah, where Satan is seen standing at the right hand of Joshua the high priest to accuse him (Zechariah 3:1-2). Satan is rebuked by God, and the high priest is then clothed in new robes instead of filthy clothes. The purpose of Satan here is to harm the high priest and corrupt the worship of God, but again we see he is under God's authority, and his work is reversed upon the order of the true King of the world.

The Gospels

After his baptism but before his public ministry, Jesus was led by the Spirit into the wilderness to be tempted by the devil (Matthew 4:1). The devil, otherwise called the "tempter" in this passage, attempted to lure Jesus with three different temptations. He encouraged Jesus to use his power to short-circuit his plan of salvation. In all three cases, Jesus responded using words of Scripture. He successfully resisted the temptation and remained sinless and set in the direction of the cross, and the devil left him.

The Synoptic Gospel writers noted that Jesus spoke of the devil as a strong man with whom he is in conflict (Matthew 12:22-32)[24]. When the Pharisees accused Jesus of casting out demons by the prince of demons, Jesus responded using a logical argument. Why would Satan cast out Satan? It makes no sense for Satan to be divided against himself and be working against his own kingdom. No, Jesus instead claimed to cast out demons by the Spirit of God. He explained using an illustration. Imagine you wanted to enter the home of a strong man and plunder his goods; you could not do this unless you first disable the strong man. The reason Jesus could cast out demons was that Satan had been bound up and was helpless to prevent Jesus casting out his evil spirits. Satan might be the king of the underworld, but Jesus is far greater than Satan.

On several occasions, Jesus spoke of the evil intent Satan has for the world. Satan is the one who works against God's purposes. The devil is the one who sowed the weeds in the parable of the weeds (Matthew 13:39) and the one who snatched away the seed that fell on the path in the parable of the sower (Mark 4:15). Despite the devil's evil plan, when he speaks of the day of judgment to come, Jesus makes it clear that the devil and his angels will face eternal punishment (Matthew 25:41).

Jesus teaches that there are two basic realms in the world: you are either children of God or children of the devil (Matthew 13:38). In what was most definitely an offensive speech, Jesus labelled some Jewish leaders as "children of the devil" despite being physical children of Abraham (John 8:44). Interestingly, Jesus even labelled Simon Peter as Satan when he rebuked Jesus for speaking of his coming suffering and death (Mark 8:33). By this, he meant that Peter was acting in line with the purpose of the devil, attempting to divert him from his chosen course that would lead to the cross[25].

Satan is described as either entering Judas to lead to his betrayal of Jesus (Luke 22:3) or putting it in Judas' heart to betray Jesus (John 13:2). Yet Judas faced punishment for his sin. This is a similar situation to David's census in the Old Testament. The devil has the power to tempt and deceive, but the one who gives into the temptation is guilty of sin. It is not the temptation that causes sin (or else Jesus would be sinful), but the succumbing to temptation is sinful.

The rest of the New Testament

The language of the two realms, the realm of light and darkness, of God and the devil, can be found throughout the rest of the New Testament as well. For example, Paul tells King Agrippa that his ministry aims to have people turn from darkness to light and from the power of Satan to God (Acts 28:18). This also explains the times when Paul speaks of handing people over to Satan (1 Corinthians 5:5, 1 Timothy 1:10), meaning that those who are not in the church and under God's lordship are in fact under the lordship of the devil.

Satan's great threat to Christians is the threat of temptation to sin. Married couples are encouraged not to withhold sex from one another because Satan might tempt them for their lack of self-control (1 Corinthians 7:5). Forgiveness of others is encouraged in order to avoid being outwitted by Satan (2 Corinthians 2:11). Letting the sun go down on your anger might give an opportunity to the devil (Ephesians 4:26-27). The risk of temptation is real, and Christians are encouraged to live in a way that realizes the risk and avoids situations where it is difficult to resist.

The devil also continues to work in other ways to oppose God's purposes in the world, even after Jesus' death and resurrection. Paul attributed his thorn in the flesh to a messenger of Satan sent to harass him (2 Corinthians 12:7). Satan hindered Paul from visiting the Thessalonians (1 Thessalonians 2:18). We are not told exactly what the thorn and the hindrance were, but they are attributed to Satan's work. Believers were also warned about the continuing work of the devil (1 Peter 5:8, Revelation 2:10).

Despite the threat, as in the gospels, believers were also encouraged that the devil can be resisted (James 4:7), his work would not continue to threaten forever (1 Peter 5:10), and that God would crush Satan under their feet (Romans 16:20). Satan has real power even after Jesus' victory on the cross, but Jesus is the king of the world, not Satan. The devil is an enemy to be wary of but not one to despair of ever defeating.

Other passages about the devil in the Bible

There are two critically important passages that refer to the devil but are frequently debated as the words used are not as clear as the other texts we have looked at already.

The serpent in the Garden of Eden

It is commonly accepted that the serpent in the Garden of Eden is the devil, though it is never actually described in that passage as being Satan. However, the action of the serpent in tempting the woman to take the forbidden fruit is consistent with what we know of the devil from other passages. The serpent receives a curse from God for his behaviour, but Adam and Eve are still held responsible for their actions and receive a curse for them[26]. In John's vision in Revelation 12:9, Satan is also called "that ancient serpent...the deceiver of the whole world", so it is reasonable to conclude that the serpent is Satan himself. We can see that the serpent is still under the rule of God and subject to God's judgment, despite being opposed to God's work in the world.

We are never told where the serpent in the Garden came from. How did something so evil find a place in God's perfect creation? Although it is not stated directly, it is fair to assume that the fall of Satan must have occurred prior to the creation of the world. When read against passages like Ephesians 1 which speak of God choosing his covenant people before the creation of the world (Ephesians 1:4), we can conclude that Satan's tempting and Eve's falling into sin were not surprises to God. He knew in advance this would happen and already had a plan for salvation (Genesis 3:15).

As an aside, this shows us the extent of God's grace towards us. When God made the world, he knew what was going to happen. He knew about the events that would lead him to send his one and only Son to die as a criminal on a cross. And yet God made the world in any case. He knew the cost and was prepared to pay it for the salvation of his people, to his glory.

The Lord's Prayer

When Jesus taught his disciples to pray, he gave them the words of what we know today as the Lord's Prayer. In the last sentence of the Lord's Prayer, we read, "and lead us not into temptation, but deliver us from evil" (Matthew 6:13). As footnotes in all major English translations will attest, this final word 'evil' can also be translated as "the evil one." In Greek, the word evil is a definite noun, not just a general sense of evil. When compared to the previous sentence that speaks of temptation, it seems reasonable to translate it "the evil one." The devil is behind temptation and believers are encouraged to pray for God to rescue them from Satan, knowing that God is the one who rules the whole world including the devil[27].

What does the devil do?

Allan Chapple summarizes the devil's work in the world in the most memorable way: the devil works by error and by terror[28]. In the book of Revelation, we read that the danger facing the churches included teaching as opposed to the gospel (Revelation 2:24) and terror (Revelation 2:10). This is consistent with what we have seen in our survey of the Bible. The devil tempts people to trust in something other than God (as in Genesis 3), or he works more overtly, threatening the people of God (Job 1-2, 2 Corinthians 12:7, 1 Peter 5:8). This can come about in any number of ways; we don't need to just beware of talking snakes or little red beings with devil horns![29] Believers need to be aware that they are susceptible to being tempted especially if they are struggling with self-control (1 Corinthians 7:5) or anger (Ephesians 4:26-27).

Jesus uses the same two categories for the devil's work in John 8:44 when he labels some of his Jewish opponents as "children of the devil." Jesus calls the devil a murderer and a liar, again using the two categories of force and deception.

Where did the devil come from?

The serpent simply appears in the Garden in Genesis 3 with no backstory. The reality of evil in the world and the work of Satan and evil spirits is assumed throughout the Biblical account;

however, the Bible has no detailed account regarding the fall of Satan and the circumstances around this.

In Isaiah 14:12-15 and Ezekiel 31:10-14 we read two accounts which compare the impending fall of world superpowers to the fall of Satan. It is not clear how much of these passages can be taken as a literal description of the events around the fall of Satan given that they are both poetic illustrations. However, Paul also alludes to the devil as being under condemnation for being puffed up with deceit (1 Timothy 3:6-7) which matches the basic teaching of Isaiah 14. It seems reasonable to conclude that at some point in history, Satan rebelled against God in his pride and was cast down in response. We are not told the details in the Bible; it is enough for us to know of the devil, his threat to us and his ultimate doom.

The devil is not alone in his malicious work. There are references to the devil 'and his angels' (such as Matthew 25:41) and many references to evil spirits, showing us that Satan is the head of an army opposed to the work of God. Satan's fall, therefore, was not the fall of one being but many.

What power does the devil have?

When we see advertising that uses cartoon devils to sell used cars or to convince us to eat ice cream, it is a sign that the devil has lost the ability to inspire fear in the modern imagination. Claiming that the temptations that Satan offers might lead you to be a little poorer or a little fatter are not anything to take seriously.

This popular portrayal seriously downplays Satan's influence. Satan has real power in this sinful world, but this is something we need to be careful not to overstate. The real world is not like a Star Wars movie, with the good side of the force and the dark side of the force in constant battle and uncertainty over which side will win[30]. God is in complete control over all creation including the devil. This is a consistent theme throughout the Bible passages we have looked at.

That being said, the devil has power for a time now to tempt and persecute people. Believers are warned in multiple places that the devil might tempt them through people they trust such as teachers in the church (2 Corinthians 11:14) and through signs and wonders (2 Thessalonians 2:9).

Satan should not have the power to terrify us, for if God is for us, who can be against us (Romans 8:31)? We who trust in Jesus know that the victory is already certain and one day Satan will be crushed (Romans 16:20) and thrown into the lake of fire (Revelation 20:10). Satan does not truly have the power over the world that he claimed in Matthew 4. Believers even now have the ability to resist the devil (James 4:7).

God can use the plans of the devil for his own good purposes

The devil makes plans for evil, but God's purposes for the good of those who love him still stand. We see this in a few different episodes in the Bible. In the opening chapters of Job, it is clear that Satan intended harm for Job. He desired that Job would lose his fear of God and instead curse God (Job 1:9-11). God permitted Satan to act as he desired, but he used the same things Satan intended for Job's harm to bring about increased understanding and blessing for Job. The devil cannot thwart God's good purposes through his actions; even the evil actions of Satan can be used as part of God's bigger plan for the world.

We see something similar in 2 Corinthians 12 when the apostle Paul speaks about his "thorn in the flesh" (v7). Paul describes this thorn as a "messenger of Satan" (v8), something the devil used to harass him. However, in the same passage, he describes this thorn as having a positive benefit for him in the greater purposes of God. Even though the thorn was something he desperately asked for God to remove from him, Paul understood that this affliction kept him from being conceited and helped him to understand that God's power is made perfect in weakness (v7,9). Again, something the devil used with evil intent was used by God for a positive purpose in Paul's life.

This is an example of a wider issue in the Bible which is put most memorably in Genesis 50:20 when Joseph reflected on the actions of his brothers to sell him into slavery in Egypt. They meant evil for him, but God meant it for good. This returns us again to a major theme of this book: God is in control of everything that happens in this world. Even the work of the devil cannot thwart the plan of God. God can use the things intended for our harm by the devil for his good purposes.

How should believers think about Satan?

After reading about the power of Satan and his work in the world (considering what was done to Job, for example), many believers are terrified. In some branches of the Christian church, believers are taught they must engage in spiritual warfare with the devil and live in constant fear of his ability to do terrible things to them. We need to take comfort in the New Testament teaching on this topic.

Yes, the devil has power. But we serve the One who has the ultimate power over all things including the devil. Christians can stand firm against the schemes of the devil when clothed with truth, righteousness, the readiness that is ours through the gospel, faith, salvation and the word of God (Ephesians 6:10-16). We can resist the devil, and he will flee from us (James 4:7). Despite the devil prowling around like a roaring lion looking to devour us, he can be resisted by remaining firm in our faith (1 Peter 5:8-11). However much power the devil has, if we belong to Jesus nothing can separate us from the love of God (Romans 8:38-39). We need not be terrified of what the devil might do to us. It is possible to resist the devil if you are a believer.

It is important to say something at this point about temptation. As we have seen, one of Satan's common threats to us is the temptation to sin and turn our backs on God and his love. That has been his way since the beginning (as in Genesis 3). There is a difference between temptation and sin, and just because we will be tempted in many ways does not mean that we must fall into sin. The Bible encourages us when it comes to facing temptation, that we will not be tempted beyond what we can bear (1 Corinthians 10:13). We can avoid situations that make us more open to giving into temptation (such as anger Ephesians 4:26-27 and lack of forgiveness (1 Corinthians 2:11). Believers have the Holy Spirit dwelling in them (Romans 8), and, of course, we have the power of prayer. The prayer that Jesus encouraged his disciples to pray includes asking our Father, who loves us, to deliver us from the evil one (Matthew 6:13). Our God, who understands what it means to be tempted (Hebrews 4:15), knows what we need and is pleased to grant prayers such as these.

Thinking the devil has irresistible power, some have claimed that the devil made them do something, and they are not responsible for their actions[31]. On this point, the Bible is crystal clear. We are always responsible for our sin. Yes, there might be circumstances that led to our sin. Yes, we might have a weakness in a particular area. Yes, the devil may well be behind the temptations we face. But if we sin, we sin ultimately because we have decided that instead of serving God we want to serve ourselves (James 1:13-14). David was tempted by Satan in his census (1 Chronicles 21:1) but was held responsible for his actions. Satan filled the heart of Ananias to lie to the Holy Spirit, but Ananias was judged for his own sin (Acts 5:3). Each of us is responsible for our own sin. All of us are guilty and desperately need the salvation only offered through Jesus.

Believers need not be terrified of the devil. We need to be alert to the risk we face every day, but not defeatist, believing that falling into sin is something that is inevitable. We worship the one who has already won the decisive victory over Satan and who will one day oversee his permanent destruction.

A life trusting Jesus is a life free from the accusations of the devil

As we have already seen, the word 'devil' means 'accuser'. Part of the devil's power in encouraging error is that he accuses people of sin. This power is taken away from Satan through the victory of Jesus on the cross. In Colossians 2, Paul explains that one result of Jesus' resurrection from the dead was that he cancelled the record of debt that stood against believers (v14). With no debt remaining, because Jesus has paid it all, the spiritual rulers and authorities are disarmed (v15). Satan has nothing to hold against us, for our debt is fully paid, and there is nothing left to accuse us of (see also Rev 12:10-12).

This has wonderful implications for Christians. There will be times when we feel so unworthy of God, that we are so sinful that there is no way that God could ever love us. At those times, we can remember that these accusations are false and have no basis. Yes, all Christians are unworthy of God, but our debt is fully paid if we trust in Jesus as our Saviour and Lord. We can have assurance of salvation because it is due to the work of Jesus and not our worthiness. The devil might try to convince us of our debt, but the reality is that he is disarmed, and the debt is paid.

Another way that the devil might work against us to make us fear death (Heb 2:14-15). If we don't trust in Jesus as our Lord, there would be reason to fear death and judgement; the writer to the Hebrews describes this as being subject to lifelong slavery (v15). Christians don't need to fear death and what follows, for Jesus has destroyed the devil who had the power over death (v14). Instead of living in fear of death or striving to ignore the reality of that we will die one day, believers can be confident as we face the future. We don't face an uncertain future but a certain one. Our future is controlled by Jesus our Lord, who has defeated Satan. The devil no longer has the power to accuse us or bring the fear of death into our lives; he is a vanquished foe.

The strong man is bound: the ultimate encouragement

Frederick Leahy puts forward a useful illustration to help believers consider the reality of Satan's position now. He compares it to thunder and lightning. In reality, thunder and lightning occur at the same time, but from where we stand, we see the lightning much sooner than we hear the thunder because light travels faster than sound. God's victory over Satan occurs at the cross: that is when the critical battle was won (John 12:31, 16:11). We live in the "time-lag between the lightning and the thunder, between Satan being cast down and the hearing of the crash of his fall. With God, there is no such gap, and at the final judgment, when time will have ended, we shall see for ourselves that the cross stood at the heart of history and that there Satan was in fact cast out"[32].

Satan, for all his current power, is a defeated foe. As Martin Luther put it in his famous hymn[33]:

> *A mighty fortress is our God,*
> *a sword and shield victorious;*
> *he breaks the cruel oppressor's rod*
> *and wins salvation glorious.*
> *The old evil foe, sworn to work us woe,*
> *with dread craft and might*
> *he arms himself to fight.*
> *On earth he has no equal.*
>
> *No strength of ours can match his might!*
> *We would be lost, rejected.*
> *But now a champion comes to fight,*
> *whom God himself elected.*
> *Ask who this may be: Lord of hosts is he!*
> *Christ Jesus our Lord,*
> *God's only Son, adored.*
> *He holds the field victorious.*
>
> *Though hordes of devils fill the land*
> *all threat'ning to devour us,*
> *we tremble not, unmoved we stand;*
> *they cannot overpow'r us.*
> *This world's prince may rage, in fierce war engage.*
> *He is doomed to fail*
> *God's judgment must prevail!*
> *One little word subdues him.*

God's Word forever shall abide,
no thanks to foes, who fear it;
for God himself fights by our side
with weapons of the Spirit.
If they take our house, goods, fame, child, or spouse,
wrench our life away,
they cannot win the day.
The kingdom's ours forever!

Questions for reflection or discussion

- Satan has often been added to the list of mythical creatures and villains, in the same category as dragons and goblins. How should it change your view of the world to believe that Satan really exists?

- Should Christians be terrified of the power of Satan? Why/why not?

- Is there any danger from being too interested in Satan?

- Should Satan often be mentioned in Christian prayers? Do you include regular prayers to be delivered from the evil one? Why/why not?

- One of Satan's chief weapons is temptation. How, practically, might Christians resist temptation? What kind of things might you do to resist giving into temptation?

Chapter 3: Evil Spirits and Demon Possession

"There are two equal and opposite errors into which our race can fall about the devils. One is to disbelieve in their existence. The other is to believe, and to feel an excessive and unhealthy interest in them. They themselves are equally pleased by both errors and hail a materialist or a magician with the same delight."

C.S. Lewis, The Screwtape Letters

In the modern Western world, the idea of someone being possessed by evil spirits seems like a relic of the past. It is easy to try to rationalize or explain this away using modern categories. Perhaps the people Jesus interacted with were simply mentally ill? Perhaps the people back then didn't understand science or medicine and so labelled everything they couldn't explain as being due to evil spirits? As we have discussed in previous chapters of this book, that kind of explanation will not do. It does not take the Biblical accounts seriously enough. Jesus labels them specifically and repeatedly as evil spirits and gives a great deal of focussed teaching about them. What is striking in these accounts from a modern perspective is that everyone at that time accepted that being possessed by an evil spirit was a possibility and a separate concern to being ill. The Gospel writers often include demon possession and sickness in lists of things Jesus heals, indicating that people could determine the difference between the two. The demon-possessed people also often know information about Jesus that no-one else knows, something that cannot easily be explained away without reference to the supernatural.

People who have grown up in Eastern cultures, even in today's modern world, generally have less trouble accepting the reality of demon possession.

It appears to be more common in certain cultures and is well documented.

If you do believe that demon possession and evil spirits are real, that can lead to different concerns, such as being terrified by the possibility of being possessed by demons yourself. I have always been an avid reader and have read widely since I was a kid. Many books have made me think, some books have made me laugh, but only one book I have read has terrified me. It was "The Exorcist." I read it as an older teenager. As I already believed in evil spirits from my reading of the Bible, the vivid descriptions in that novel kept me awake through to the early hours of the morning.

Thankfully, demon possession has not been part of my personal experience. However, the weirdness of it must not lead us to dismiss it or to be terrified of it. We need to examine what the Bible says about this so Christians can consider helpful ways of thinking about this and be assured once more of the kingship of Jesus.

A brief overview of evil spirits in the Bible

Although the bulk of references on this topic can be found in the New Testament, evil spirits are not a phenomenon that only appeared at the time of Jesus. In Judges 9:23, God sent an evil spirit between Abimelech and the leaders of Shechem with the purpose of bringing discord and mistrust between them. In 1 Samuel, there are several times that Saul is said to be afflicted by a harmful spirit from God (1 Samuel 16:14). This spirit tormented Saul and was identified by his servants as being an evil spirit and not a disease; the playing of David's harp soothed the situation. This spirit led Saul to rave and throw spears at people he trusted (1 Samuel 18:10), to act against what he would usually do. Likewise, in 1 Kings 22, the prophet Micaiah tells of "lying spirits" coming before God and making a case for how they could lead Ahab to his death; God is identified as sending these lying spirits in the mouths of the false prophets in Ahab's court (1 Kings 22:18-23). In all of these Old Testament cases, the evil spirit is described as leading to bad consequences for the one being afflicted.

What is striking about all of these Old Testament references is that they are all explicitly stated to have come from God. This kind of language makes us uncomfortable. We'd like to ascribe control over the good things in life to God but are reluctant to also ascribe to God control over the evil things. We need to be careful here. The Bible does not describe a dualistic world, a world where good comes from God and evil comes from the devil, where good and evil are in a battle neither can win. That idea is more at home in the Confucian philosophy of yin and yang or the dualistic world of Zoroastrianism. God is in control of everything that happens, both good and bad. We already noted that in Job when we thought about Satan. It is true that Satan desires evil for people and not good, but it is also true that Satan cannot do anything without permission. The same applies to the evil spirits in the Bible.

Demon possession in the Gospel accounts is common. It is a condition recognized by those in that society when they see it. We are not told anything about where the evil spirits come from, but their existence and active operation is assumed[34]. There are passages where diseases and demon possession are listed together, suggesting that they could be differentiated (such as Luke 7:21, 8:2, Acts 5:16). Instead of trying to summarize the numerous mentions of demon possession in the Gospels, for our purposes it makes sense to focus on perhaps the most famous one: the case of Legion. In Mark's Gospel, which is known for its brevity, the episode with Legion takes up twenty verses, showing how important this incident is for understanding the power of Jesus.

Legion, who we read about in Mark 5, was a man who was terribly afflicted by unclean spirits[35]. He lived in the tombs, a place regarded as 'unclean' according to Jewish law, and with superstitions dreaded by most. The fact that he had been bound indicates that he had caused harm not only to himself but to the local community as well. His strength was superhuman, and he was dedicated to self-harm. His was a terrible and isolated existence. When Jesus came to his region, this man ran to him, fell down before him, and correctly identified him as "Son of the Most High God" (v7). The demons who possessed the man recognized the power and identity of Jesus and knew this was not a conflict that could be won. They only wished to negotiate that they not be tortured but rather cast into nearby pigs. Jesus gave them permission to do so. This was not a bargain won by the unclean spirits, but a concession allowed by Jesus, possibly because it visually indicated the power and quantity of the spirits who had inhabited Legion[36]. The result of all of this was that this previously uncontrollable man was "clothed and in his right mind" (v15). This drastic change scared the locals who begged Jesus to leave the area, and it led to the man himself begging to leave with Jesus but instead becoming an effective local evangelist (v20).

It is interesting to note that the locals are described as being afraid when they saw the man after he was healed. This is fear of Jesus, not of Legion. Here was a man who was possessed by demons, and he is completely healed at a command from Jesus. This was unheard of and showed the great power of Jesus. Whoever could command demons in this way was someone to fear. The power of Legion was something they were familiar with and were managing; the power of one who so easily restored this man was terrifying to them.

This episode with Legion has many similarities with other cases of demon possession we see in the Gospel accounts. The evil spirits were always intent on harming their host (Mark 9) and they had special knowledge about the identity of Jesus (Mark 3:11-12). These spirits completely controlled the person to the point that they use the voice of the person. This shows us that we are dealing with a supernatural force and not a medical issue.

No person who was healed from demon possession was ever rebuked by Jesus for sin. Being possessed by an evil spirit was not something that the host was responsible for, and any actions taken while possessed were not the conscious actions of the one afflicted. That puts demon possession in a different category to giving into temptation, for which we are responsible, as we saw in the previous chapter.

Exorcism in the Jewish world of that day existed, but it was a long and convoluted process with no guarantee of success. Those in the crowds that observed Jesus' casting out of evil spirits were not just amazed that this could be done; they were amazed that it could be done so easily. Jesus' fame spread in part because of this power

(Mark 1:27-29). Jesus' exorcism ministry could be summed up in the words of Matt 8:16: "he cast out the spirits with a word." At times, Jesus even cast out evil spirits from a distance (Mark 7:25). This was no evenly-matched fight; this was a laughably one-sided contest. As we noted in the previous chapter, the fact that the evil spirits could be so easily cast out by Jesus showed that he had bound the strong man, Satan, and was plundering his possessions. It was a sign of the power Jesus had over the powers of darkness and their impending ultimate doom.

Jesus also offered direct teaching on evil spirits in Matthew 12. Casting evil spirits out of a person did not guarantee they would not return. In fact, seven spirits may return to inhabit the place left by one (v45). If those from whom evil spirits were cast did not come to trust in Jesus, they were in no better position than before. Just like with his healing of disease that only delayed death and did not prevent it, the casting out of evil spirits was symbolic of the greater victory, not the end in itself.

Jesus even granted his disciples authority over evil spirits, leading to them being involved in their own exorcism ministry (Mark 6:7). A key episode in Mark 9 showed that their capacity for casting out demons was not as effective as Jesus' power. A man with a child who was overcome by seizures due to an evil spirit asked the disciples to cast the demon out, but they could not. Jesus rebuked the spirit and cast it out immediately. When asked about this, Jesus told his disciples that this kind could not be driven out by anything but prayer[37] (Mark 9:29). It was important that the disciples realized that the power to cast out demons was only from God and not from their abilities or status.

The ministry of the apostles in the book of Acts was accompanied with many signs and wonders including the casting out of evil spirits (demonstrated by Peter in Acts 5:14-16 and Philip in Acts 8:5-8). This casting out led to great joy, for the evil spirits only caused destruction and harm. In one memorable case, Paul and his companions were followed by a servant girl who had a spirit of divination (Acts 16:16). The spirit that afflicted her identified Paul and his companions accurately and supernaturally, similarly to the spirits in the Gospels. Paul cast the spirit out, and the girl could no longer tell fortunes, meaning a loss of income for her master.

Acts 19 records the account of the seven sons of Sceva, children of a Jewish high priest who were practising as itinerant exorcists. They had apparently had some success in casting out spirits using the name of Jesus (despite not recognizing him as Lord). However, an evil spirit confronted them, leapt on them and overpowered them. The spirit did not recognize them; the name of Jesus they invoked was not a magical formula for exorcism. The name of Jesus is not some magic word that can be invoked for exorcisms, but he is the Lord with whom a personal relationship is needed. This episode makes us recall the somewhat frightening words of Jesus that some will claim to have cast out demons in the name of Jesus yet they will not be welcomed by Jesus on the last day (Matthew 7:22-23).

With the many accounts of evil spirits and demon possession in the Gospels and Acts, we might expect some direct teaching on this in the letters of the New Testament. Instead, we are given no instructions on how to carry out exorcisms or how to avoid being possessed by a demon. There are no warnings about evil spirits. Although it is difficult to make an argument from silence, it would be reasonable to assume that if this was a debatable issue in the early church, it would have been mentioned in one of the letters. Either demon possession was not a concern to the early Christians, or it was an issue that was agreed upon and did not need an apostle to correct or make a judgment on it.

Different words used of demon possession

We read in the Bible of situations where evil spirits are sent to people (Judges 9:23), they trouble people (Luke 6:18), people can be said to "have" them (Mark 1:23) or be afflicted by them (Acts 5:16), but the Bible never actually uses the term demon possession. For this reason, some scholars prefer the word demonization[38]. For our purposes in this book, I believe demon possession is a reasonable term to use as it conveys the reality that people afflicted in this way are controlled by a spirit intent on harming them.

As for the terms used of the spirits themselves, they are referred to as "evil spirits" (such as in Judges 9:23 and Luke 8:2) or "unclean spirits" (as in Matthew 10:1 and Mark 3:11). The writer of 1 and 2 Samuel refers to them as "harmful spirits" (1 Samuel 16:14) while the writer of 1 Kings uses the term "lying spirit" (1 Kings 22:2). At other times, they are called "demons" (Luke 8:2). Whatever title these beings are labelled with, they are associated with the devil as his possessions (Mark 3) and being under his control (Revelation 16:13).

Does demon possession still happen today?

I wish I could say that demon possession was limited to the time of Jesus and the apostles and such a phenomenon could never happen anymore. Regretfully, I cannot. There is much evidence that demon possession as described in the Bible continues to this day. There are always many people who give evidence of first-hand experience or belief in the paranormal, and it would be naïve to dismiss all of these accounts of ghosts, poltergeists and the like to mass hallucination or deception.

While at university, I met a young man who had been converted out of a background in the occult. I asked him what it was that first interested him in Christianity. He said that when he read the Gospels, it was not the miracles and casting out of demons that grabbed his attention, but Jesus' teaching and authority. The reason that the miracles and supernatural things did not surprise this young man was that he had seen many strange things with his own eyes. He had seen objects float across rooms and the work of evil spirits that had been actively summoned and encouraged. It is a reminder that there are many things in this world that we cannot see, and not all of them are good or benign. Ultimately, it was a wonderful work of the grace of God to change this young man's heart to see the truth about the power of Jesus.

Missionaries who have served in Papua New Guinea frequently report meeting people who have been afflicted by demons. Christian workers in Africa often enter a tribal worldview where people live their lives in abject fear of demons and curses, and where witchdoctors have a large and real influence on their communities. Western missionaries who have entered this kind of culture have often made the mistake of thinking that all of this evil spirit emphasis is nonsense and that there is no place for the supernatural and evil spirits at all. Biblically informed missionaries should approach this topic with caution rather than presuming that evil spirits are not at work in the communities they have come to serve[39].

It would be easy to fill this chapter with blood-curdling eyewitness accounts of demon possession, but this would be unnecessarily disturbing for us. I think it is enough to make it clear that demon possession is a real phenomenon and not simply something from the Bible that can be explained away or presumed to be no longer relevant to us today.

The question this raises for those of us who are less familiar with evil spirits is: why don't we see more demon possession in modern, Western cultures? The best answer I have heard comes from a theology lecturer I had the privilege of studying under who had spent time in Pakistan. His theory was that cultures founded on Christianity seem to have a significantly lower incidence of demon possession, pointing again to the power of Jesus. However, over time, as Western culture slides further from its Christian roots and people turn to the occult and other belief systems, I believe this is likely to change.

Another related concern is whether non-Christian people are randomly afflicted by evil spirits, or whether certain practices might increase their susceptibility to being afflicted in this way. I would think that the high prevalence of demon possession cases in the third world, where interaction with the spirit world is encouraged via festivals and animistic cultures, would suggest it is not random. As will be explored in a later chapter, we do not want to mess around with the world we cannot see.

Should Christians be afraid of evil spirits?

This is where the practical value of this chapter comes in. Christians do not need to fear evil spirits, for they trust in the One who defeated Satan and who rules the whole world. The Holy Spirit is God himself who dwells inside all believers (Acts 8:17, Romans 8:9) and we do not need to be afraid that some evil spirit will move in and control us for evil. Christians cannot be possessed by evil spirits. Remember how easily Jesus cast out every evil spirit who came across his path? He who is with us is so much more powerful than anyone or anything that is against us (Romans 8:31). Because of this, Christians do not need to fear that anything, including "powers," can separate us from the love of God in Christ Jesus our Lord (Romans 8:38).

I once spent time with a man who, due to his mental illness, was obsessed at times with the fear that evil spirits would afflict him. I remember praying fervently with him, encouraging him that he was a much-loved child of God, someone who had the Holy Spirit, and someone who was protected from anything the evil one might bring against him. This prayer visibly calmed down a man who was highly agitated prior to this. Don't underestimate the power of prayer and the One we pray to.

Martin Luther had much to say on the topic of demonic activity and evil spirits. He clearly believed in the continuing activity of such spirits, but his consistent advice was to pray fervently to the One who was clearly more powerful than the evil spirits. A pastor asked Luther for advice on poltergeists, claiming that Satan was hurling pots and pans at his head. Luther replied, "Let Satan play with the pots. Meanwhile, pray to God with your wife and children and say, 'Be off, Satan! I'm lord in this house, not you. By divine authority, I'm head of this household, and I have a divine call to be pastor of this church[40].'"

Evil spirits and their impact continue, more evident in some parts of the world than others. But in any place, Christians do not need to be afraid. These spirits might well be more powerful than us, but through Jesus, we have access to the Father who hears our prayers and controls all things (1 John 4:4-6).

We can see this most clearly in 1 Peter 3:22, which states that "angels, authorities and powers" are subject to Jesus who sits in heaven at the right hand of God. Or, as Paul notes in Ephesians 1:21, Jesus has ultimate authority over all rule, power and dominion that exists in this age or the age to come.

Should identification of evil spirits and exorcism be a part of Christian ministry and counselling?

There are some streams of the Christian church that focus on deliverance from evil spirits, either those afflicting the one being counselled or perhaps those influential in their family or city. Those who practice these things often seek to know the name of specific demons and require detailed confessions and prayers by the one being helped.

This kind of practice has no Biblical precedent and is contrary to what Christians today should be devoting themselves to. Jesus did not command exorcism or any ministry focussed on deliverance from demons in the Great Commission (Matthew 28:16-20). The apostles saw their ministry as focussing on the preaching of the Word and prayer (Acts 6:4). Although Jesus and the apostles were involved in casting out evil spirits, it was not the main focus of their activity nor something they are ever described as seeking out. As Wayne Grudem points out, no-one in the New Testament summons a territorial spirit, demands information from demons, says we should teach or believe things from demons, or says that we need to break demonic strongholds in a city[41]. Even Daniel, who had spiritual battles revealed to him, was not urged to get involved in this spiritual realm.

The practical danger of these deliverance ministries is that they overemphasize the influence of evil spirits on the lives of believers and do not encourage confession and personal responsibility for actions. It is too easy for us to ascribe our own sin to spiritual forces, but that didn't work for Eve in the Garden of Eden, nor will it work for us.

Of course, those who come face-to-face with demon possession on the mission field will always need to pray for God to work to help those so afflicted. But the fundamental ministry, even in that situation, is prayer and the Word of God. Casting out demons does not necessarily lead to someone being converted (Luke 11:24-26). Even if someone could practice an effective exorcism ministry, that would not necessarily lead to more people trusting in the true King.

Matthew 7:22-23 also reminds us that it is possible to chase the glamour of exorcism and miss the far more important aspect of knowing and trusting in Jesus. We should remember that Christianity is fundamentally about trusting in the One who has won the victory for us, not about us saying exactly the right formula or following the right procedure. Anything that focusses on our actions and not the victory Jesus has won will lead to us being distracted from the gospel rather than deepening our faith.

A reminder: the evil spirits are no match for Jesus

As it is so important, I will repeat it again here: evil spirits are no match for Jesus. If you trust in Jesus as your Saviour and Lord, you are trusting in the One who defeated the devil and his power on the cross. You have the Holy Spirit living in you, and you need not fear that you will be possessed by some demonic force. You can be certain that nothing, not even the scariness and power of evil spirits, can separate you from the love of God in Christ Jesus your Lord (Romans 8:38).

Questions for reflection or discussion

- Why do you think evil spirits and supernatural evil forces feature so heavily in horror movies and books? What is it about these themes that can be so terrifying?

- Do you think that ghosts and other unexplained supernatural things are due to evil spirits, or is there some other explanation?

- Have you ever witnessed or heard of modern demon possession? If so, how did this experience make you feel? Why?

- Why do Christians not need to fear demon possession? How does understanding the power of Jesus help us here?

Chapter 4:
Spiritual Warfare

The 'Spiritual Warfare' section of your average Christian bookshop delivers quite the experience. There are hundreds of books to choose from, and based on the variety of books available, they sell particularly well.

A cursory glance around my local Christian bookshop yielded books ranging from a bonded leather edition of "Prayers that Rout Demons and Break Curses" to many guidebooks on how to engage in spiritual warfare, how to cleanse my house from territorial demons, and other how-to books that promised to help me win the battle against the invisible enemy. In even more niche markets, there were books that offered spiritual warfare guides specifically for women, and Bibles where all the commentary notes were on the topic of spiritual warfare. I don't know how you feel about these kinds of books, but they deeply sadden and anger me. The foundation of so many of them runs completely against Biblical Christianity as if we needed to say magic words or special prayers lest we be dominated by evil powers. That sounds like traditional pagan religion to me and not Christianity where we serve a victorious and omnipotent Saviour and Lord.

There is something right about us being aware of and possibly concerned about the unseen spiritual world. However, we must not obsess over it, seeing spirits lurking behind everything and feel that it all depends on us and our ability to use the right technique to defeat those powers. Christians can have far more confidence in the world than that because of the One we have confidence in. As the apostle John writes, "we know that everyone who has been born of God does not keep sinning, but he who was born of God protects him, and the evil one does not touch him" (1 John 5:18).

Considering that you can buy entire Bibles with commentaries on spiritual warfare, you might expect that there were thousands of references to people actively resisting or standing up against unseen, spiritual forces. This is not the case. The Bible is not silent on the issue of spiritual warfare, but it is not as dominant a theme as many books would make it seem. Unlike other chapters in this book, we will focus our attention on only one key passage: the armour of God passage from Ephesians 6. This is a famous passage and for a good reason (and not only because it lends itself to memorable craft in a Sunday School lesson for children!). Spending time in this passage will help us to have real hope as we face unseen enemies.

The context: the flow of the book of Ephesians

Ephesians 6 is right at the end of the book of Ephesians. That might sound like a pretty insignificant point to make, but it always helps us to think about the context a passage is found in. Paul's letter to Christians in Ephesus is wonderfully encouraging and is split into two main sections. The first three chapters explain what all believers already have because of Jesus – an extensive list! We have "every spiritual blessing in the heavenly places" (1:3), redemption, forgiveness of sins, adoption, an inheritance, and certain future hope. And all of this has already been done for us. Chapters one to three are full of encouragement and blessing.

For example, look at this section from the end of Ephesians 1:

> *"[Christians have so much] according to the working of his great might that he worked in Christ when he raised him from the dead and seated him at his right hand in the heavenly places, far above all rule and authority and power and dominion, and above every name that is named, not only in this age but also in the one to come. And he put all things under his feet and gave him as head over all things to the church, which is his body, the fullness of him who fills all in all."*
>
> (Ephesians 1:19-23)

The scope of what Jesus has done and the authority he has is incredible. Paul is all-inclusive in his language. Christ is at the right hand of God above all rule and authority. He is head of all things. As I have repeatedly noted, that includes Satan, evil spirits, angels, any spiritual authority as well as human authorities.

The second half of Ephesians, chapter 4 to 6, gives us practical instructions as to how we should live as people saved by Jesus. Where the first three chapters are almost entirely descriptive, there are a lot of commands and instructions in the last three chapters. Paul gives instructions on living as saved people, being part of a church community, and the implications for marriage, children, and slaves.

You could sum up the message of Ephesians with the phrase "be what you are." If you trust in Jesus, you already have so many blessings because Christ is already the victor and King. Because of this, all Christians are called to live life as saved people, in a thankful response to God's grace and Jesus' victory.

Then when we come to our focus passage in Ephesians 6, Paul placing instructions on spiritual warfare in this context means that these actions are part of our response to Jesus already giving us every spiritual blessing. Our salvation does not depend on praying the right prayer or resisting some evil spiritual being. The victory is won. Ephesians 6:10 says we are to be strong in the Lord, in the strength of his might. We are not to think that it is all about our strength but God's strength. We are to be what we are: saved people standing confidently in the blessings that have already been won for us.

Ephesians 6: the whole armour of God

This passage is about spiritual warfare, for want of a better term, but let's not get too carried away with the warfare imagery. Paul encourages believers to put on the full armour of God in order to be able to stand against the schemes of the devil (v11). He then repeats the same concept again in v13. The key phrase here is "to stand firm." Paul does not urge believers to defeat evil spirits or regain ground claimed by territorial spirits. That is not his purpose. He is helping equip the believers in Ephesus to stand firm. To remain where they are. To not be tempted and terrorized by the work of the devil and his servants. These are enemies that are beyond us to defeat; that is one reason we need Jesus! What Christians are called to do is to stand firm.

Paul then tells these first-century Christians that "we do not wrestle against flesh and blood, but against the rulers, against the authorities, against the cosmic powers over this present darkness, against the spiritual forces of evil in the heavenly places" (Ephesians 6:12). For much of the history of Bible interpretation, this has been read as a reference to the unseen world of angels and demons. This seems the most natural way to read this passage, especially as the last phrase of v12 locates these powers "in the heavenly places." The devil is real, there are real spiritual threats to believers, and there are things that believers are urged to do in response to these threats.

The verses that follow this outline the armour of God itself, a most memorable picture of how Christians can be equipped for this spiritual battle. Note first that all except one of the items that are described are defensive in nature. The emphasis here is on defending ourselves against the devil's schemes, not on attacking spiritual enemies.

The belt of truth and the breastplate of righteousness (v14) are not expanded upon but are quite self-explanatory. Believers are to be equipped with truth and clothed in the righteousness they have received from God. We are to be clothed in appropriate clothes. It is true that believers are still sinners, but we have put off the old self and put on the new self. Striving to live a life pleasing to God is an essential part of the Christian life. We have been clothed in Jesus' righteousness[42], and now we strive to live a life that matches our new clothes.

The armour of God also includes shoes: the

readiness given by the gospel of peace (v15). This could involve the readiness to evangelize[43], but in the context of Ephesians, it relates more widely to how we live (as in Ephesians 5:15-16). Knowing the gospel of grace means that our priorities change, and we want to make the most of the time that has been given us to serve God in different ways. Having shoes like this shows that Jesus is not just theoretically important but is instead our Saviour and Lord who changes how we live.

In v16, when Paul speaks of the shield of faith, he once more refers directly to the "evil one." This shield is effective for extinguishing the flaming darts of the evil one. What can this mean? On the one hand, it means that the devil is actively seeking to harm believers. That is something we have already seen earlier in this book. Satan actively desires to damage Christians. In that context, we need faith. This doesn't mean that if we don't believe strongly enough, we cannot resist the devil. As so often stated in Scripture, our faith is our trust in Jesus and what he has done, not reliance on the strength of our belief.

What saves Christians is not the fact that we have faith, it is who our faith is in. Those of other beliefs, including atheists, have faith too. The Christian faith truly saves people, and not because those who call themselves Christians believe strongly enough; people are truly saved because Jesus defeated Satan and paid for sin through his death and resurrection. All we need is faith the size of a mustard seed (Matthew 17:20). The emphasis has to be on God's grace and not our faith, on God's faithfulness and not any incredible strength of belief. Therefore, the shield of faith means that we are relying not on our own abilities to resist the devil but on the power of Jesus in whom we have our faith. Holding this shield means that we do not engage in spiritual warfare by saying or doing the right things; we resist Satan by trusting in Jesus. These instructions hold true in "all circumstances" (v16).

The helmet of salvation is the last piece of armour that Paul mentions in this passage, and he doesn't expand upon it. The thing that marks us and completes our armour is the fact that Jesus has saved us. That is what protects our heads. It is not because of our stubborn resistance but because the work Jesus has done for us is effective.

Interestingly, in all this armour there is only one weapon listed: "the sword of the Spirit, which is the word of God" (v17). This weapon is listed together in the same sentence as "praying at all times in the Spirit," showing us that the Spirit works through the Scriptures and prayer. The only real way we can resist the devil is knowing our Bible, meditating on it day and night (as in

Psalm 1), and praying that God would help us resist temptation (as instructed in the Lord's Prayer). This is also the model Jesus gave to us when he resisted the devil in the wilderness (Matthew 4:1-11), always responding to temptation with a relevant Scripture passage. We can't identify lies and false teaching if we don't have any knowledge of the truth as explained in the Bible.

A friend of mine used to work as a bank teller in the USA. As part of their training to recognize counterfeit notes, the tellers were given tasks intended to get them used to the feeling of regular banknotes in their hands. The more familiar you are with the original, the less likely it is that you will be fooled with a copy. That lesson applies to how Christians should know their Bibles. The temptations we are likely to face from the devil are encouraging us to think or act or speak in ways that go against God's will for us. It is by knowing God's word that we will be able to recognize these temptations for what they are. Knowing our Bibles well is our weapon against such deceptions.

Paul ends this section of Ephesians with a call to "keep alert with all perseverance" (v18). This lines up with the advice of the apostle Peter when it comes to the devil (1 Peter 5:8). We need to be realistic about the power of the devil and our own frailties and sin. We need to constantly remember our armour, that we are reminded that Jesus has won salvation for us and equipped us to stand firm. We need to know our Scriptures and pray, trusting God, for while we are unable to defeat the devil and his schemes, our mighty God is not.

The Ephesian Christians are then urged to pray for the perseverance of other believers through the world and for the spread of the gospel, especially in Paul's missionary work. This is not a change of topic from the armour of God section, but a continuation. The implication is that the devil, the enemy of God, will act to oppose Christian perseverance and gospel proclamation. Yet this truth need not overwhelm us, for in Jesus we can pray to the Father for help. Satan is powerful, but God had defeated him. Prayer is an important part of resisting the devil and encouraging the work of God in the wider world.

This is an important reminder to those who are involved in preaching or evangelizing. Once more we must be humble and realize that clever preaching, good illustrations, and clear logic are not the ultimate weapons in saving people. We need to be faithful to God's word and pray for it to be received by good soil. Otherwise, it is too easy for preachers and leaders to feel self-important and think by their own efforts they can change hearts and defeat the devil instead of trusting in the One who actually won the victory.

Is there a danger in being too focused on spiritual warfare?

I believe that living in constant fear of evil spirits and the devil can be distracting for our faith. Feeling the need to pray and act at all times to resist and defeat unseen evil forces can overwhelm our lives. It can mean that we become focused on our efforts instead of the completed work of Jesus on the cross. It is so easy to think that we need to read the latest book on spiritual warfare, or just pray harder; else the devil will come at us in ways that we cannot resist. That does not line up with what the Bible says at all. Paul assures the Christians in Corinth that they will not be tempted beyond what they can bear (1 Corinthians 10:13) and the same is true of us. Jesus is King. The devil has been defeated, and not by us.

Seeing evil spirits lurking behind every corner can also lead to a life that is full of unnecessary fear for sensitive Christians. There are things that go bump in the night. Satan and evil spirits are real, and temptation and terror are real weapons used by the devil. We must remember, however, that we serve a risen Saviour who even now works by His Spirit to protect us. We must not live in fear of that which has already been defeated but rejoice in the victory that Jesus has already won.

Missionaries who serve in cultures that are dominated by the fear of evil spirits report something similar in these pagan settings. When life becomes driven by encouraging good spirits and repelling evil spirits, one aspect of life that is lost is personal responsibility. Instead of accepting that poor outcomes might be due to sinful or unwise behaviour, Papua New Guinea tribespeople will instead attribute them to the work of evil spirits. This will lead to rituals and sacrifices but no attempt to change their own behaviour. Christians must not fall into this trap. We face troubles in life for a wide range of reasons. It could be the work of unseen spiritual forces, or the presence of sin in the world more generally, or a result of our unwise personal choices, or that God is refining us by his Spirit. If we simplify the world into only the impact of spiritual forces on our lives, we are not faithful to the diversity of the Scriptures and the world God has made.

The letters of the New Testament are full of direct instruction on things believers are to work on: unity in the church, witnessing to unbelievers, our behaviour in relationships, and using our gifts to build others up, among many others. It is right to be aware of the world we cannot see, but it is unwise to focus so much on this that we do not work on being godly in our lifestyles and serving Jesus wherever we have been placed.

Wayne Grudem helpfully points out that the emphasis in the New Testament is on telling people not to sin and how to live lives of righteousness, and gives very little instruction on resisting demonic activity.[44] There is no instruction anywhere to cast out a "spirit of disunity" or "spirit of selfishness." No-one in the New Testament summons a territorial spirit, demands information from demons, or says that we need to break demonic strongholds in a city.

Don't feel that defeating spiritual forces is something you need to do; Jesus has won the decisive victory already. Don't replace the good news of the gospel that leads to freedom with a life of fear. If you trust in the true Lord of the world, of everything seen and unseen, you need not fear what is frightening (1 Peter 3:6).

Questions for reflection or discussion

- Why should we be wary of books that instruct us to say special words or prayers to fend off evil spirits?

- Should Christians expect to be the target of spiritual attacks from the devil and evil spirits? Why/why not? If so, what form might these things take?

- How does knowing your Bible well help with resisting the devil?

- Prayer is a cornerstone of resisting the devil and his work. Why is prayer so central? Do you find yourself praying for help with resisting the devil?

- Can you explain away bad decisions and actions as being due to the influence of evil spirits? Why/why not?

Chapter 5: Don't Mess with the Unseen World

Witchcraft and the occult[45] used to be viewed by most people as the domain of troubled or 'evil' people and was associated with midnight meetings, graveyards, pentagrams, animal sacrifice, and heavy metal music. Times have changed. Western culture has turned from regarding the occult with revulsion to fascination and openness with the topic. There are many popular TV shows featuring witches, characters such as Lucifer, or which generally focus on supernatural themes. For a materialistic society, our TV guides and most watched lists on Netflix reveal a stubborn interest in the world we cannot see.

Some are tempted to do more than merely watch TV shows or read supernaturally-themed novels; they want to influence or tap into this unseen world. Most local markets offer some kind of tarot card reading or fortune-telling service. You can easily find someone who will offer to read your tea leaves or your aura. You can even find people willing to connect you to loved ones who have died, or who offer services to remove unwanted ghosts from your home.

Although this fascination with the unseen world is relatively recent in Western popular culture, for much of the world and much of world history people have sought to influence the spiritual world. African cultures often feature witch-doctors who rule villages with the threat of curses. Traditional Asian cultures will offer sacrifices to ancestors to encourage good outcomes in their lives and avoid bad ones. People who lived in ancient Rome were known to carry amulets to ward off evil spirits and seek out oracles at places like Delphi to ask what might happen in the future (for a fee, of course)[46].

How should Christians think about these things? If we know that there are such things as angels and demons, Satan and evil spirits, is it wrong for us to seek out information from the spiritual world? Is there any possible harm to our faith when it comes to consulting fortune tellers or psychics? As usual, we should go to the Bible first to see what guidance God has for us there before drawing our conclusions.

The Old Testament

As early as the book of Genesis, we are shown a society where people put great value on signs and dreams as a way of knowing what will happen in the future. When Joseph was sold by his brothers into slavery in Egypt, he found himself in trouble with the law. While imprisoned, two of his fellow prisoners had dreamed but were downcast as there was no-one to interpret their dreams for them (Genesis 40:5-8). Their assumption was that dreams are meaningful and can be interpreted to reveal the real truth. Joseph told these men that all interpretations belong to God and then proceeded to interpret the two dreams, foretelling the future of the dreamers correctly.

At a later stage, Joseph was summoned to Pharaoh to interpret the dreams of the king. The king was angry that the magicians and wise men of Egypt could not interpret them (Exodus 41:8), implying that these people were routinely sought out to assist with this. Joseph gave the correct interpretation, and God used this to bring him to power in the court of Pharaoh to save many. This shows us that although God can send dreams which reveal the future, magicians and the like cannot always work out the meaning.

Dreams and their interpretations also feature in the book of Daniel where Nebuchadnezzar's dreams are accurately interpreted by Daniel when his magicians and enchanters cannot do it (Daniel 2:10). Even the magicians admitted that they needed divine help to interpret such things. Dreams might be one way information from the unseen world enters our usual world, but they are rarely of great use to us unless God himself reveals their true meaning. God occasionally revealed his purposes to prophets through dreams, but they were never a significant ongoing means of informing his people of what was to come.

On a similar note, when Moses and Aaron originally were sent to Pharaoh with signs to perform, we see that the Egyptian wise men and sorcerers in the royal court could indeed match some of the signs themselves (Exodus 7:11). They had real power, but a lesser power than God had given to Moses (Exodus 7:12, 8:18).

Whilst many of the nations mentioned in the Bible were known to use diviners and fortune-tellers (Deuteronomy 18:14), God repeatedly commanded his people not to use these means to contact the unseen world. Like so many other aspects of Canaanite culture, seeking the future through magical means was something the nation of Israel was called to avoid. They were to put their trust in God and what he revealed to them through the law and the prophets. The law of Moses outlaws mediums and sorcerers in no uncertain terms, such as we see in these passages:

> *"A man or a woman who is a medium or a necromancer shall surely be put to death. They shall be stoned with stones; their blood shall be upon them."*
>
> (Leviticus 20:27)

> *"There shall not be found among you anyone who burns his son or his daughter as an offering, anyone who practices divination or tells fortunes or interprets omens, or a sorcerer 11 or a*

> *charmer or a medium or a necromancer or one who inquires of the dead, 12 for whoever does these things is an abomination to the LORD."*

(Deuteronomy 18:10-12)

There is nothing vague about these prohibitions, nothing open to interpretation. Using any kind of means to discover the future or contact the dead was outlawed. As God's chosen people, God communicated through his prophets and required them to trust him for their futures, something distinctive compared to the other nations.

Jesus later summarized the first and greatest commandment using words from Deuteronomy 5, that "you shall love the Lord your God with all your heart and with all your soul and with all your mind" (Matthew 22:37). God's people were only to serve God and were limited to what God had told them.

As the kingdoms of Israel and Judah slid into a terrible state far from their God, at times we are told that some of the Israelite kings sought answers from occult practitioners rather than the prophets and the law. This is universally condemned in the books of 1 and 2 Kings. For example, King Ahaziah sought an answer as to whether he would recover from an illness from the god of Ekron, a neighbouring country (1 Kings 1:2). His messenger was intercepted by the prophet Elijah who then pronounced a severe judgment on the king for seeking answers in the wrong place. Other kings even went as far as to set up temples to foreign gods in their cities and installing new priesthoods which worshipped the sun and the stars (Ezekiel 8:16). They were hedging their bets, trying to influence the unseen world through any possible means, and showing a lack of trust in the power of the one true God.

The Old Testament is abundantly clear on the act of seeking answers about the present or the future from the unseen world: it is outlawed. God's people must have nothing to do with magicians, astrologers, mediums, or any person who attempts to influence the unseen world in a way God has not approved.

A longer passage on this theme: Saul and the witch of En-Dor

While we completed an overview of Old Testament teaching on this topic, one episode from the life of Saul deserves special attention. We read about it in 1 Samuel 28. Saul, for all his problems, had upheld the law on this point: mediums and necromancers were banned from the land (v3). This had not completely eliminated people who were involved in such things; there must have still been a market for their services.

Saul was facing a great battle with the Philistines which he knew he could not win, and the prophet Samuel was dead. He was desperate for guidance in this matter, but God had not spoken to him through any priests or dreams or prophets. In his desperation, Saul sought out a medium[47] for guidance, a method he knew full well was banned by the law he himself had enforced. As with most black-market services, if you know where to look, you can find what you want, and Saul soon discovered who to speak to. There was a medium who lived in a place named En-dor (v7).

Suitably disguised, something necessary for a man who was a head taller than any in Israel, Saul visited this medium, assuring her that she would not be reported for what she was about to do. He asked to speak to the spirit of the prophet Samuel. When the medium saw Samuel, she cried out in a loud voice and immediately knew that her strange visitor was Saul himself (v12). This bears reflecting on. Speaking to spirits was the trade of this woman, yet she was surprised and afraid when she saw Samuel. This vision was different from what she was used to seeing.

Saul responded to the description of the spirit of Samuel with respect as he would have if Samuel was present in person (v14). Samuel rebuked Saul for disturbing him to seek answers that God had withheld from him. Saul does, however, get guidance about the future from the spirit of

Samuel: Israel would lose the coming battle, and Saul and his sons would die (v19). Saul was terrified of what was coming and needed to be encouraged to eat before he left.

This is the lengthiest passage detailing the work of a medium in the Bible, and it answers some questions and poses others. It is clear that Saul was wrong in seeking answers from the dead. However, he was still given answers through this means, even if they were answers he did not want to hear. Does this mean that mediums are real? Perhaps they are a valid means for seeking information? Definitely not. I believe that the summoning the medium did here was not her usual experience; God chose to use this unusual means of communication this one time to send a message to Saul. In that sense, it is not unlike God using a burning bush or a donkey to speak to his people at specific times and places.

The passage about the medium at En-dor cannot be used to support the use of mediums or sorcerers, as this would contradict the clear teaching of the law. Throughout Scripture, we are told that once someone has died, the living are not to attempt to communicate with them (see 2 Samuel 12:23, Luke 16:26).

The New Testament

Magic and interest in the magic arts were still alive and well at the time of Jesus. Matthew reports that magi from the east came to worship the newborn king (Matthew 2:1). Although their point of origin is not reported in the Gospels, Babylon has traditionally been thought to be their homeland due to the use of the word 'magi' and their known interest in astrology[48]. Once more, we have a situation somewhat like the medium at Endor; we cannot use this passage to normalize magic or astrology. Matthew's point is that Jesus' birth is of great significance not only to Israel but to the wider world. God is using astrology, a discipline never commended in the Bible, to lead these men to the true King. Their response was appropriate, but this does not mean we should study the stars to reveal the truth about the future and world events. This is a special case.

The book of Acts, which outlines the spread of the gospel through the apostles, includes several episodes where Christians came into contact with magicians or sorcerers. It would seem that these people were commonly in respected positions as advisors to those in power through the Roman world. For example, Philip met a man named Simon in Samaria, who practised magic and amazed the people there (Acts 8:9). However, even Simon is amazed by the signs that Philip performed as part of his ministry, knowing they were beyond his abilities. He wanted these abilities for himself but was rebuked for his greed and wrong motives. In another instance, Paul meets a man named Elymas in Cyprus, who is described as a "magician" and a "Jewish false prophet" (Acts 13:6). Elymas opposes the message of Paul and is struck blind at Paul's command; the combination of Paul's message and this action on such a powerful and revered advisor led to the local proconsul believing in Jesus (Acts 13:12).

Possibly the most powerful conflict between the gospel and the magic arts happened in the city of Ephesus. This city was known for its embrace of the magic arts. When a great many people in that city responded to the preaching of the gospel, they confessed and rejected their former practices (Acts 19:18). It was clear to them that their former work in the magic arts was contradictory to the gospel of Jesus. They publicly disposed of their magic books to show their repentance. Although these books were expensive[49], they did not seek to sell them and enable others to follow their teachings, but rather burned them at great cost.

The New Testament, unsurprisingly, maintains the same consistent teaching on these issues as the Old Testament. Believers in Jesus must not be involved in the magic arts. The power of the risen Jesus is greater than any power found elsewhere.

Who are practitioners of the occult actually communicating with?

You might have noticed that in all these Bible

references there has been nothing explicitly teaching that those involved with the occult are communicating with the devil. They are accessing some kind of power and can do minor wonders, but the source of that power is not named. This should cause us some concern. Those involved in witchcraft may not always know where their power and information is coming from, other than that it is from a realm they cannot see or fully understand. Perhaps some did attribute their power to Satan or evil spirits. Whatever the source, we can know it is opposed to the one true God as seen in Elymas and the repentance of the converts in Ephesus.

The fact that we see the occult always shown in opposition to the gospel would mean that logically the supernatural power behind it must be attributable to Satan or evil spirits. We have seen already that the dark unseen world has real power and that we underestimate it to our peril.

It is not politically correct in our modern age to say that the worship of other gods is not valid or real. However, the Bible is abundantly clear on this issue: there is only one true God who is the God of everything. This means that sacrifices and communication directed to other gods must logically be given to either no god at all (Jeremiah 10:8-10) or to evil spirits. Paul explicitly refers to this in 1 Corinthians 10. When instructing believers on the issue of offering food to idols, he says that "what pagans sacrifice they offer to demons and not to God" (v20). The application that arises from this is clear: God will not tolerate the worship of anything other than himself. Syncretism, the thinking that all gods are the same, has no place in Biblical thinking, despite being a popular view in both ancient times and our modern world.

How is using prayer and the Bible different from accessing the occult?

At this point, you might think that the Christian opposition to fortune-telling and the occult seems a little hypocritical. After all, don't Christians try to influence God and the future through prayer? Don't Christians rely on a special book that gives them the supernatural information they could not otherwise know?

These are good questions. It is too easy for people who believe one thing to simply dismiss those who believe in something else. There needs to be a good reason why prayer and the Bible are in a different category to fortune-telling, and there is.

Christian prayer is often thought of as trying to twist God's arm to do something for us he would not otherwise do. That is not how Jesus spoke about prayer. He described it as speaking to our Heavenly Father who loves us and already wants to bless us. Christians are encouraged to ask for anything they want in the same way that a child might ask their parents (Matt 6:8). This, however, is not the same as manipulating God. Behind every Christian prayer is the knowledge that God may have different plans for us than we imagine for ourselves. Parents often know better than their children, and when it comes to God, he always knows better than us. Christian prayer is completely different to fortune telling as we present our request to God, knowing they might well be denied or delayed, while fortune-telling is about getting information from sources apart from God so as to know the future and change our lives to suit ourselves.

Similarly, the Bible is a book that reveals supernatural information to us, information we would not otherwise know. We need God to tell us what he is like, as we cannot simply work it out for ourselves. God has revealed a great deal to us in the Bible. What he has not revealed are the kind of things people seek to know through the occult: what decisions we personally should make now, such as whom we should marry, and where we should live. Christians are instructed to grow in our understanding of God and his world and our place in it, and as we do this, we are to make wise choices with what is known to us. This element of personal responsibility is different from seeking answers directly from a fortune teller. In the end, this will lead to us growing in our faith rather than being spoon-fed information as we go through life.

The logic of serving the one true God is simple: we must not seek other sources of supernatural information (Isaiah 8:19-20). While all of us would like God to clearly provide the information about our next major life decision to us, most often this does not occur. We need to be satisfied with this level of knowledge. There is always some uncertainty as we face the immediate future, but we trust that our Heavenly Father has it under control and is working it out for our good (Romans 8:28). Our future plans are known to God but not always to us, and we are to be satisfied with that. As frustrating as that might be, we are not to seek to find more information about the future God has not revealed to us.

Is all of this medium and fortune teller stuff a hoax?

The usual position of someone who has never had any contact with the occult is that it is all a big con. Those who offer these services must be charlatans and fakes, people who can observe their customers and tell them what they want to hear. It is a profession that it is quite possible to fake because it is difficult to check whether what someone 'sees' is real or not. We also see this in published horoscopes which are so vague that they can be made to fit any circumstance. I am always likely to meet a stranger or do familiar things, for example, and if I believe it to be true, I can see amazing things in the vague words.

This is not a modern problem. In many cultures, people have been wary of people offering to tell the future because so many of them are not real.

Let's not be so quick to rule out the whole enterprise as lies and rubbish peddled by charlatans. When God outlawed mediums and sorcerers in the law, he did not say that these things were to be avoided because they were not real. God said they were inappropriate for his people to be involved in. That is a big difference. The magicians in Egypt and Babylon did have power. The people in Samaria had good reasons to be amazed at Simon the Sorcerer. The servant girl Paul met in Acts really could tell the future. There is real power to be found in these places, but this power is specifically outlawed by God.

Just because there are many mediums and magicians who are fake doesn't mean it is all fake. There is power to be found in the occult.

Is there any harm in dabbling in tarot or visiting a medium?

Absolutely! What might seem like harmless fun is something outlawed in God's word and has the potential to damage our faith. The Bible's language used regarding these things is telling: they are an abomination (Deuteronomy 18:12) which we must flee from (1 Corinthians 10:14).

Many who have grown up in rural villages in Africa have grown up in fear of the local witchdoctor; other from villages in rural Malaysia have been terrified of the medium who controlled their community. There are real reasons for such fear. Although Christians can be confident that Jesus is Lord, even of the spiritual world, we must not then assume that these people who claim to contact the spirit world have no power at all.

Perhaps popping into the booth to have your palm read or checking your horoscope in the newspaper seems like a bit of light entertainment. In reality, it undermines your trust in God alone. It means that you are seeking to know things God has not told you in ways God has expressly forbidden. This is something that should not be messed around with.

Likewise, beware of superstitions that claim that you can influence your life for good or evil, such as using crystals, wearing amulets or avoiding certain numbers in your house, hotel room or car license plate. These things are especially common in eastern cultures, as are looking to auspicious dates to do certain things and placing certain items in your house to drive away bad luck and attract good luck. Trusting in these things is an attempt to manipulate your future by appeasing or avoiding evil spirits or some other part of the unseen world. Being a believer means trusting in God alone for your future; these types of beliefs put too much emphasis on the impact of the spirit world on our lives and our attempts to influence it. Jesus is the king, more powerful than any evil spirit, and we need not live in fear of what we cannot see if we are a child of God.

Can we take part in festivals and cultural events involving spirits and the dead?

In some Eastern cultures, significant annual and family celebrations have a component of contact with the world we cannot see. For example, the firecrackers that are set off during Chinese New Year celebrations are intended to scare away the evil spirits. Some festivals celebrate times when those who have died can have temporary contact with the living, such as the Mexican Day of the Dead. Funeral rites in some parts of the world require a family member to offer incense to the person who has passed away. Christians who have grown up in cultures like these, especially if they have non-Christian family members who believe in these mystical practices, can find themselves having to make awkward and sensitive decisions. Can we take part in such things? What is allowable for Christians, and what is unhelpful or sinful?

There are a few issues to consider in asking these questions. Christians do not want to cause unnecessary grief to their family members who don't share their faith, but they want to be a good witness to Jesus and not compromise their own consciences. This will require wisdom rather than a hard and fast rule. Anything that intends to engage with the unseen world or involves prayer to anyone other than the true God should be avoided, while less objectionable components of festivals and family events can still be observed.

Many children of deeply religious Chinese parents, for example, have shown respect to those who have passed away at funeral ceremonies, but have politely declined to offer incense. Others have cleaned grave sites as part of annual festivals but have refrained from offering prayers to their ancestors.

Some cultural practices might need to be rejected altogether if they compromise our faith. We cannot assume that festivals are benign simply because many don't take the spiritual component of them seriously; if it involves communication with the unseen world, we must avoid it at all costs.

How much weight should we place on dreams?

Dreams are an interesting topic because they are

not something that is actively sought by the one who dreams them. However, some people place extreme importance in attempting to seek meaning in dreams thinking that they might learn information about the future.

God has used dreams quite extensively in the past to reveal the future (as in the dreams Joseph and Daniel interpreted) or to better explain current events (as in the dream Joseph had when Mary was pregnant, Matthew 1:20). I do think, however, that Christians need to be careful not to seek answers in dreams rather than in the understanding and application of the Bible.

God does not promise to speak to all believers in dreams, and the apostles in their letters do not encourage seeking answers in dreams. This alone should give us pause. If God has not promised to communicate to us in this way, we should focus on the means by which he has promised to communicate with us. God has revealed so much to us in the Scriptures which is clear and helpful.

We can also never be sure that the source of all of our dreams is God. Our dreams may be the products of our own subconscious at best or the false lies of Satan at worst. If you don't know where the information is coming from, you need to be cautious how much weight you place on that information. If God is consistent, which the Bible says he is, any dream that contradicts something in the Scriptures must not be from God. Any dream that encourages us to act against God's word or behave immorally must be rejected.

How about seeking God's will by seeking out prophets, signs, or feelings of peace?

Many believers chase after mystical experiences. They want the personal experience of a message for their specific situation. This takes a few forms. Some church traditions encourage prophetic words from certain leaders which hold a great deal of weight. Others pray for a sign (much like Gideon did) or expect to feel some kind of warmth or peace on making the right decisions.

In essence, this mystical search has much in common with the motivation behind seeking out fortune-tellers and mediums. It wants special revelation from God instead of having to apply our wisdom and God's already revealed Word. As we noted in the discussion on dreams, God does not promise such personalized information. We have been told what God is like, what we should do, and where the world is heading; with this information, we have incredible riches. Believers would be better advised to study and know their Bibles better while praying and trusting God for their futures.

Mysticism is vague and subjective by its nature. What exactly does a sense of peace mean? If we feel peace about a decision, it simply means we like and are comfortable with that decision. To then ascribe this feeling of peace to be God's revelation to us is taking it too far. As sinners, we are quite likely to feel comfortable with a decision that is opposed to God's will! We should stick to a firmer foundation rather than looking to hear more than God has told us.

Prophecy is slightly different to this, for the New Testament describes 'prophecy' as one of the gifts of the Spirit. This is a topic that is beyond the scope of this book, but for now, it will suffice to note a few quick things[50]. Prophecy is to be valued in the church and must be something intelligible and useful for upbuilding, encouragement and consolation (1 Corinthians 14:3). It may happen that someone applies the Scriptures accurately to your specific situation, giving guidance as to what you should do in a certain situation. This might indeed be valid as it has a strong foundation. But even that needs to be tested instead of simply accepted (1 Corinthians 14:29). All believers should read the Bible and meditate on it, trying to see the practical implications for their lives. That is where our attention should lie instead of seeking information from other sources.

The need to use our wisdom and God's revelation together

Maybe you have read this chapter and been a little disappointed. You want God to be more personal for you and give you specific information about your future and God's will for your life. That is what the fortune-tellers promise and God does not.

God has told us so much in the Scriptures, and he expects his people to use their wisdom to apply this knowledge. There are whole books in the Old Testament (known as Wisdom Literature) which are reflections about the world and life and God's word. Paul, in his letters, doesn't often just tell his readers what to do but explains it linking the gospel and logic. For example, he doesn't simply command the Corinthians to exercise church discipline in 1 Cor 5; he explains why this matters practically and in terms of the gospel. We are to think and not just be told. God wants us to think deeply about his word and its application in our lives.

Not knowing what is going to happen next is actually a blessing. We are called to serve God well today with what we know. It is quite possible the future will be nothing like we expect, and this will humble us and remind us that God is God and we are not (James 4:13-17). Instead of trying to find out more information, we just need to get on with the task of serving Jesus in the time and place he has put us right now.

Magic and entertainment

We already noted that many TV shows and other

popular media have supernatural themes. Some well-meaning Christians have read the prohibitions against the occult in the Bible and have concluded that we should ban the Harry Potter books while being suspicious of the Lord of the Rings trilogy. While the motivation for this might well be godly, the application is faulty.

There may be movies and books that are best avoided. I have watched 'The Ring' before in an attempt to show my toughness in watching a horror movie; it disturbed me, and I would never recommend anyone watch it. Similarly for the book and movie 'The Exorcist.' There is no godly reason to get involved in these types of entertainment.

The problem with wanting to ban books like Harry Potter is that they are fictional and use the medium of magic as a way of telling a story. Some of the most influential novels written by Christians in modern times have had themes of magic or fantasy (such as C.S. Lewis' Narnia series and Tolkien's Lord of the Rings). These books can help us understand the presence of good and evil in the world. The magic is not the main theme but a medium presented in such a way that doesn't promote it as a means to run your life. Those who read these books do not end up convinced that they should use magic to influence their futures; they are clearly a work of fiction.

As with so many issues, where individual Christians choose to draw the line on the place of magic in entertainment will be different. Each of us has a different conscience. What is fiction and not a problem for most may be a temptation for others; each should be convinced in their own mind[51].

It might be helpful to ask yourself some honest questions as you decide whether a particular form of entertainment is something you should enjoy. Will watching this build me up? Is this something that would be beneficial to my faith? Is this something that will cause me unnecessary fear and trouble my mind?

There is a world we cannot see. It is right for us to know that there is more to the world than what we experience with our senses, but something else entirely to seek to connect with unseen forces and obtain information from them. Christians are to trust that God is in control, that Jesus is more powerful than whatever other forces exist, and that he has told us what we need to know in the Scriptures. Let's face the future with confidence because Jesus is Lord. It is humbling and helpful for us not to know all the personalized details of our future. We just need to get on with serving God as best we can, wherever he has put us. We might not know our exact future, but it is more important to trust the One who does.

Questions for reflection or discussion

- Do you think that most fortune-tellers and mediums are real or fake? Why?

- Many would say that superstition like avoiding certain numbers and dates is just cultural and not such an important issue. Do you think this kind of superstition is a problem for Christians or not?

- How is not knowing exactly what will happen in your future helpful for your faith?

- Do you personally find it a problem for your faith to watch television shows with supernatural themes? Why/why not?

- Christian books on spiritual warfare are best-sellers at the same time that general Bible knowledge in the wider Christian community is at a historic low. Why are so many Christians more interested in special revelation from God and less on studying what God has revealed to us in the Bible?

Conclusion: Having Confidence in the Darkness: Jesus Is Lord

Angels and demons are real. Satan is not an imaginary bogeyman. Demon possession is not some ancient misrepresentation of mental illness. We also know that all of these unseen beings are far more powerful than we are.

The natural response to these truths would be to stay awake at night, terrified by forces beyond our control. That response is perfectly logical. There is a reason why demon possession, exorcisms and the occult feature heavily in horror movies. There is much for us to fear.

Thankfully, Christians do not need to look out for evil spirits behind every rock or fear that demon possession might strike us helpless. This is not because we have some sort of special spiritual ability, technique or magic words that will drive away and conquer those who would harm us. Christians can have great confidence against unseen evil forces because Jesus is our Lord. Jesus showed his power over the devil and evil spirits repeatedly during his earthly ministry and defeated them for all time with his decisive victory on the cross. We might not be more powerful than the devil and his angels, but our Master is.

The universe is not involved in an eternal struggle between good and evil where either side could win. That might make a wonderful Star

Wars movie, but the Bible teaches there is one true God who controls all things. Everything created, both seen and unseen, is under his command. Nothing can separate those who believe from the love of God, including the powers of the unseen world.

This is the consistent message of the Bible. In the Garden of Eden, the devil led people into sin, but God foreknew this and had a plan to rescue them. Job was tested by the devil in terrible ways, but this was under the direction of God to teach and ultimately bless him. Evil spirits knew supernatural things about Jesus and could harm their human hosts, but Jesus cast them out easily with only a word. Christians are told to expect temptation and opposition from the devil but are also reminded that it is possible to stand firm and resist the devil so he will flee from us. We know from Revelation that the final battle will be over almost as soon as it began, with the people of God living in peace with God forever free from the power of sin, death and the devil. God is in charge of the world, not the devil.

There are many things about the unseen world we cannot know. The Bible hints at guardian angels. There are passages that speak of cosmic conflicts between angels and demons in the book of Daniel. I wish we could know how all of this works, but God in his wisdom has not told us.

All of this investigation into angels, demons,

Satan and spiritual warfare is fascinating, but we need to take care that it doesn't distract us from our main task. We are to serve God and seek to know him through the Scriptures that he has given to us. We are to pray and work on our holiness. We are to stand firm and make every effort to resist temptation, especially when we are at our weakest. We cannot blame our sinful behaviour on the reality of the devil but must confess our sin and take personal responsibility for it. We are to be grateful that our Father controls multitudes of angels and will protect us until Jesus returns, but not feel we need to communicate with angels.

The one true God that we worship is the Creator and King of the whole world. Even the parts we cannot see. That is wonderful news.

Acknowledgments

Firstly, I would like to thank God. It is God who has acted to save me through the work of Jesus, and who by his Spirit continues to mould me after his image. My prayer is that this book is used to help people see the majesty of God and the importance of the victory Jesus won on the cross.

I would like to thank my wife, Andrea, who is now incredibly familiar with the content of this book. She has patiently listened to my excited ramblings about new discoveries on this topic and has refined my thinking in many places. She has also helped me a great deal with editing my manuscript.

My three children have been patient with me working on this book. My prayer is that they come to know the victory of Jesus deeply for themselves and not fear what they cannot see.

I would like to thank the congregation of All Nations Presbyterian Church, who first heard much of this material in a sermon series. Their comments and perspectives from a range of cultures have been enlightening.

This is a stronger book due to the review and comments from Allan Chapple, Honorary Research Fellow and Former Senior Lecturer (New Testament) at Trinity Theological College, Perth, Western Australia and Tim Thorburn, Western Australia Regional Director for the Australian Fellowship of Evangelical Students (AFES) and Executive Officer of the Perth Gospel Partnership (PGP). I humbly thank them for their encouragement and wise feedback.

Endnotes

Introduction: The world we cannot see

[1] To be clear, I fully believe that Jesus is truly God and truly man, rose again bodily on the third day, and will return to the judge the world. I am satisfied that God is real and in three persons and controls all things. I hold to a traditional view of the inerrancy of Scripture.

[2] And this is the Gospel of Mark, which does not include the many angelic appearances around the birth of Jesus.

[3] Bolt, P. 2007, *Living with the underworld*, Matthias Media, Kingsford, p13.

[4] Unless specified, all Bible references in this book are from the ESV Bible (Holy Bible English Standard Version), copyright ©2001 by Crossway, a publishing ministry of Good News Publishers. Used by permission. All rights reserved.

Chapter 1: Angels, the Messengers of God

[5] See also 2 Chr 32 and Is 37:36

[6] This is expressed in the ancient Apocryphal book of Enoch and popularized in the 2014 Noah movie.

[7] Chance, J.B. 2007, *Acts*, Smyth & Helwys, Macon, Georgia, p199.

[8] Thiselton, A.C. 2000, *The first epistle to the Corinthians: A commentary on the Greek text*, William B. Eerdmans, Grand Rapids, p576-577.

[9] Calvin, John (trans. Beveridge, H.) 1981, *The Institutes of the Christian Religion*, Volume 1, Wm. B. Eerdmans Publishing Company, Grand Rapids, p146.

[10] Grudem, W. 1994, *Systematic Theology: An introduction to Biblical doctrine*, IVP, Nottingham, p397.

[11] Technically, 'seraphim' only occurs without the definite article. It is a description of what they are like rather than a name or a title (Motyer, J.A. 1999, *Isaiah*, Tyndale, Intervarsity, Nottingham, p78).

[12] Noll, S.F. 'Thinking about angels', in Lane, A.N.S. (ed.) 1996, *The Unseen world: Christian Reflections on Angels, Demons, and the Heavenly Realm*, Paternoster, Grand Rapids, p1-27.

[13] The recent book by Michael Heiser, 2015, *The Unseen Realm: Rediscovering the supernatural worldview of the Bible*, explores the many references to a spiritual council of angels in the Bible. This is beyond the scope of this book which is an introductory overview to the topic of angels and demons.

[14] McPartlan, Paul 'Angels' in Hastings, A., Mason, A and Pyper, H. (eds.) 2000, *The Oxford Companion to Christian Thought*, Oxford University Press, Oxford, p16.

Chapter 2: Satan, the Deceiver

[15] Matthew 13:39.

[16] Page, S.H.T. 1995, *Powers of Evil: A Biblical Study of Satan & Demons*, Baker Books, Grand Rapids, p65.

[17] For a helpful outline of deliverance ministry teaching, along with a Biblical critique, see Wright, N.G. 'Charismatic Interpretations of the Demonic', in Lane, A.N.S. (ed.) 1996, *The Unseen world: Christian Reflections on Angels, Demons, and the Heavenly Realm*, Paternoster, Grand Rapids, p149-163.

[18] John 14:6.

[19] *The Usual Suspects*, 2011, JL Entertainment.

[20] Ash, C. 2014, *Job: the wisdom of the cross*, Preaching the Word series, Crossway, Wheaton, p39.

[21] Frame, J. 2013, *Systematic Theology: An introduction to Christian belief*, P&R publishing, Phillipsburg NJ, p774.

[22] Page, S.H.T. 1995, *Powers of Evil: A Biblical Study of Satan & Demons*, Baker Books, Grand Rapids, p105.

[23] God "governs the world by the means of and through the agency of a multiplicity of supernatural powers, *some of whom are evil.*" Ash, C 2014, *Job: the wisdom of the cross*, Preaching the Word series, Crossway, Wheaton, p41, italics in original.

[24] This passage is included in Matthew, Mark and Luke.

[25] Keener, C.S. 1999, *A Commentary on the Gospel of Matthew*, William B. Eerdmans Publishing Company, Grand Rapids, p635.

[26] Page points out that despite Satan's power and temptation, there is nothing in Genesis 3 that contradicts the sovereignty of God or the responsibility of humans for their own sin. Page, S.H.T. 1995 *Powers of Evil: A Biblical Study of Satan & Demons*, Baker Books, Grand Rapids, p123.

[27] This is also consistent with Jesus' statement in Luke 22:31 where Satan demanded to sift Simon

Peter as wheat but Jesus prayed for him that his faith would not fail.

[28] Chapple, A. 2013, *A Gospel Pageant: A reader's guide to the book of Revelation*, Mosaic Press, Preston, p27.

[29] The depiction of the devil with horns may be based on the description of the dragon with horns in Revelation 12, but the goat legs possibly refer to the pagan worship of the god Pan. It is in literary works like Dante's Inferno from the fourteenth century that we start to see what most modern people would recognize as the devil: a being with horns, goat legs and bat wings.

[30] The religion in Star Wars is based on Zoroastrianism, an ancient religion from Persia.

[31] For example, the South African cricketer Hansie Cronje who was convicted of corruption once used this defence for his actions.

[32] Leahy, F.S. 1975, *Satan Cast Out: A Study in Biblical Demonology*, Banner of Truth, Edinburgh, p30.

[33] Luther, Martin, translation © 1978 *Lutheran Book of Worship*, administrated by Augsburg Fortress. Used with permission.

Chapter 3: Evil Spirits and Demon Possession

[34] McClelland, S. E. 'Demon, Demonization' in Elwell, W.A. (ed.) 2001, *Evangelical Dictionary of Theology*, 2nd Edition, Baker Academic, Grand Rapids, p333.

[35] When asked his name, the man replied, "My name is Legion, for we are many." This does not mean he was possessed by 10 000 spirits (the size of a Roman legion) but indicates a large number. This is confirmed by the fact that the herd of 2000 pigs

rushed into the sea. Pigs are not known for stampeding.

[36] This passage is full of things we would like answers to but are not told, such as what happened to the spirits when the pigs drowned, and whether it matters that the animals were unclean or not. In my approach here I have tried to avoid speculation and focussed on what Mark says rather than on what he does not.

[37] This indicates that there are different types of evil spirit, but it is not expanded upon in any other Scripture.

[38] McClelland, S. E. 'Demon, Demonization' in Elwell, W.A. (ed.) 2001, *Evangelical Dictionary of Theology*, 2nd Edition, Baker Academic, Grand Rapids, p332.

[39] You can find a more detailed expression of this in Keith Ferdinando, 'Screwtape Revisited: Demonology Western, African, and Biblical' in Lane, A.N.S. (ed.) 1996, *The Unseen world: Christian Reflections on Angels, Demons, and the Heavenly Realm*, Paternoster, Grand Rapids, p103-132.

[40] Quoted by Leahy, F.S. 1975, *Satan Cast Out: A Study in Biblical Demonology*, Banner of Truth, Edinburgh, p111.

[41] Grudem, W. 1994, *Systematic Theology: An introduction to Biblical doctrine*, IVP, Nottingham, p422.

Chapter 4: Spiritual Warfare

[42] Isaiah 11:5 lies behind this verse, where it is a description of the shoot of the stump of Jesse, who we now know to be Jesus himself. This piece of armour, like the rest, really belong to Jesus.

[43] This verse reflects Isaiah 52:7 in its description of the messengers of good news, so it would be right to note the importance of evangelism here. The immediate context from Eph 5 suggests a wider interpretation than this.

[44] Grudem, W. 1994, *Systematic Theology: An introduction to Biblical doctrine*, IVP, Nottingham, p397.

Chapter 5: Don't Mess with the Unseen World

[45] According to the Oxford Dictionary, the occult refers to "mystical, supernatural, or magical powers, practices, or phenomena".

[46] Hubbard, M.V. 'Greek Religion' in Green, J.B. and McDonald, L.M. 2013, *The World of the New Testament: Cultural, Social and Historical Contexts*, Baker Academic, Grand Rapids, p119.

[47] A medium is someone who claims to be able to communicate with those who have died.

[48] The word 'magi' is also used in Daniel 1:20, 2:2 to refer to wise men in the Babylonian empire.

[49] In fact, the cost is recorded in Acts as fifty thousand pieces of silver, an astounding sum.

[50] For a much fuller exploration of this topic, a helpful place to look is Carson, D.A. 1987, *Showing the Spirit: A Theological exposition of 1 Corinthians 12-14*, Authentic Media, Milton Keynes.

[51] This is similar to the argument in Romans 14:22-23, where Paul outlines how to deal with issues that Christians have different opinions on, like drinking wine and observing special days. When we take part in something, we need to have thought it through, being convinced it is suitable for us as a believer, else it would be counted as sin.

About the Author

Simon van Bruchem is a pastor of All Nations Presbyterian Church in Perth, Western Australia, where he has served since 2007. He completed his Master of Divinity at Trinity Theological College after a previous career as an industrial chemist. He considers it a privilege to be able to study and teach the wonderful news about Jesus from the Bible full-time.

Simon is married to Andrea, and together they parent three boys, ensuring life is consistently interesting and busy. When he is not involved with his work of pastoring the church and his family, he loves to tend to his fruit trees, play golf and read widely.

Simon blogs regularly at:

www.writtenforourinstruction.com

www.ingramcontent.com/pod-product-compliance
Lightning Source LLC
Chambersburg PA
CBHW070257010526
44107CB00056B/2494